In *Astrological Counsel* Noel Tyl presents, for the first time, a detailed inspection of the psychodynamics of the astrologer-client relationship.

His approach assumes that a productive counseling relationship is based upon *sharing* the horoscope with the client rather than a one-sided performance by the astrologer. Sensitive analysis requires that the deductions from the horoscope be corroborated through real-life observation of the client's behavior and through creative dialogue; only in this way can the proper nuance and emphasis, within the complex of horoscope configurations, be clarified. The client's experience and judgment are necessary aids in the behavioral translation of astrological symbolism—a translation required by the "psychological way of modern astrology."

The book describes knowledgeably and sensitively many diagnostic and counseling techniques, from fantasy projection to role reversal, which heretofore have been confined to formal psychoanalytic therapy. Underlying the book's approach is the concept of objectification—the special gift of Astrology, which, through the chart, lays bare the innermost recesses of the psyche to the light of compassionate analysis, and accomplishes in a flash what may take psychoanalysis months, years.

The book is filled with specific hints on establishing rapport with the client; perceiving behavioral clues; achieving clear, jargon-free communication; organizing the maze of horoscope detail so that it is useful to the client, while remaining free of the schematic approach of most texts which violate integral identity by dividing it tidily into houses and then aspects.

Throughout, it is marked by grace, charm, and humor that leaven its exalted sense of mission: to broaden the service of Astrology by seeking to modify attitudes and behavior through the objectification of the horoscope and the dynamics of sharing.

ASTROLOGICAL COUNSEL

Volume X

The Principles and Practice of Astrology

The Llewellyn Syllabus
for home study and college curriculum

The Principles and Practice of Astrology

NOEL TYL

A complete text for instruction and reference in the practice of
standard astrological methods and the psychological and
philosophical principles for analysis and application. In 12 volumes.

Volume X
ASTROLOGICAL COUNSEL

1977
Llewellyn Publications
Saint Paul, Minnesota, 55165, U.S.A.

First Edition 1975
Second Printing 1977

Llewellyn Publications
Post Office Box 3383
Saint Paul, Minnesota 55165

International Standard Book Number: 0-87542-809-6
Library of Congress Catalog Card Number: 73-19927

Printed in the United States of America

The meeting of two personalities
is like the contact of two chemical substances:
if there is any reaction,
both are transformed.

Carl Jung

Contents

Introduction

Throughout this series, we have worked intensely to relate measurements to deductions and translate the deductions into behavior. No matter how great the astrologer's skill may be, he or she needs the client's corroboration. The client's *actual* behavior must be related back to the measurements and deductions in order to establish *unequivocally* the total identity that is the horoscope.

What is established through the astrologer-client relationship is validity of measurement, balance of deductions, and level of behavior. Incisive diagnostic techniques reveal nuance and interrelationships within the identity that allow analysis and counsel to take place.

This volume examines the dynamics of the astrologer-client relationship, the artful use of perception and dialogue to bring the individual and the horoscope as close together in actual presence as is possible. The individual and the horoscope become one. Reactions build greater knowledge for the client and the astrologer. For both, the consultation is a process of learning with the goal of knowledge.

1

1

Original Sin

It's fascinating how easy it is to watch a television show, spot a guest on an interview program, and immediately declare his or her Sun Sign. It's easy because the guest can't corroborate or refute deduction, can't establish the ramifications that define integral identity.

It's fascinating how astrologers among themselves constantly are labeling this trait or that trait of someone else—or even of themselves—astrologically. Similarly, in an impersonal chat on an airplane, for example, a person with astrological knowledge will intrude into someone else's life with "What is your birthday?" or will accept the challenge with "Oh, you're an astrologer, well my birthday is such and such. What can you tell me about myself?"

All of these examples often serve only to gratify the egos of astrologers. The rationale is that the scientific dimension of Astrology will be proved by the ease and validity of the deduction. The reality is that the astrologer is trying to prove his or her own skill with the tools of Astrology. In these cases, the astrologer is performing. The performance is one-sided—the *astrologer's* side—and in this one-sidedness sharing is lost, relationship is curtailed, and dialogue is eliminated.

In an astrologer-client relationship, the tendency to perform is even more crucially present, since Astrology and the astrologer appear under test and evaluation. One-sided performance is thought to be expected. In that such ¡performance, one-sided and aggressively defensive, prevents sharing, corroboration, learning, and profitable counsel, *one-sided performance* is Astrology's "original sin."

When the astrological performer becomes over-analytical with technical jargon, he or she becomes increasingly *fatalistic.* Full service through Astrology becomes increasingly remote: one-sidedness practically eliminates the client's contribution, and fatalism denies the integrity of the client's will, the uniqueness of his identity. One is reminded of the old psychiatrist joke: Dr. A meets Dr. B and says, "Good morning." Dr. B thinks, "I wonder what he meant by that." It's the same thing among astrologers, except we tend to think we *have* all the answers: "Hi! It's a great morning, isn't it?" She must have the Moon in Sagittarius! Or a woman I overheard at an astrologers' convention, pausing to catch her breath on a stair landing: "Whew! With my Aries Ascendant, I'm always getting ahead of myself!" Or the letters written with astrological musing, like: "I'm just waiting until Uranus enters Scorpio to see what it will do to me."

These attitudes deny the potential of Astrology for self-understanding and client service. Within this volume, let us try to turn these attitudes around, to redeem ourselves from original sin by trusting our craft and ourselves and by seeking to relate the individual to the horoscope; we must not impose astrological epithets upon the integrity of the will, hopes, dreams, efforts, and fulfillment of the client.

We can begin by dedicating our astrological interview not to proving Astrology or our technique in using it, but to tallying the client's complexities with those of the drawing and the deductions, to uncovering behavior to corroborate and enrich the prepared analysis. We begin by mastering the techniques of perception and communication.

Over half of all my clients arrive for their consultation with a tape recorder. They *expect* a one-sided performance. Not understanding Astrology makes them anticipate a "reading," a recitation of things as they are, have been, and ever shall be. Immediately, I say, "Please, we won't need to record our talk together. You'll do most of the talking, and we might have to cover some very private matters. The recorder might inhibit our work together."

The important words here are "talk together," "work together." Immediately, the client is keyed to participation, to sharing, to a responsibility to cooperate in a discussion that is dedicated to full, private dialogue. This involvement immediately at the beginning of the consultation prepares the scene for the enormous diagnostic strength of Astrology: objectification (chapter 2).

Often, the client will reply, "But how will I remember it all. May I take notes?" The astrologer's answer here establishes further the professional relationship and his or her skill in managing the consultation: "I promise you that you will remember all that we learn together. We'll understand everything together. Sure, you may take notes if you want, but I don't think even that will be necessary, except perhaps at the end of our talk, when we discuss some dates in the future." This further statement clarifies the enormous responsibility for the astrologer: clear communication.

If the opportunity for the tape-recorder conversation doesn't present itself, the astrologer can easily make similar statements about "talking and working together," or "understanding everything together" in order to establish what is expected during the consultation. Dialogue will be essential; full understanding, the goal. Already, the two-sidedness of the consultation is established: the client is fascinated to be involved; the astrologer is relieved of the expectation of solo performance; a skilled professional atmosphere is established within the confidentiality of the meeting; the astrologer immediately relies on the clinical techniques of perception and communication. He has already begun to work *with* the client, rather than *at* or *upon* the client.

Perception

From the first moment that the client arrives for consultation, the astrologer's powers of observation and perception must be at their highest efficiency. The objective is to try to relate to *what is already known about the horoscope,*[1] what is now visible in the client or revealed in his initial reactions, communication, and movements. Evidence of the Sun-Moon blend (Volume III), the Ascendant, major House emphases, dominating geometry (Volume IV), and the synthesis of the major aspect configurations should be looked for to establish the relative balance of these horoscope dimensions within actual self-presentation and behavior.

This acute observation and perception begins with a study of what the astrologer presents as a stimulus for the client's initial reactions:

First, is your home or apartment comfortable? Does the scene of the consultation register your orderliness, professionalism, and the necessary privacy? Do you have arcane, mystical, or esoteric paraphernalia that might frighten or distract the client, that definitely will not help in any way during the consultation, and only serve to make you feel more like a medieval mystic? Conversely, it is important that your consultation room be maximally comfortable, have within it evidence of your knowledge (books) and organization (neatness). Your appearance must be neat, alert, and attractive—even to the point of changing a necktie, scarf, shirt, pin, dress, sports jacket, etc., to a color you know your client will appreciate (seen through the Sun Sign, with adjustment through the Moon

1. It practically goes without saying that part of "original sin" is *not* having the horoscope fully prepared before consultation. Any astrologer not fully prepared—computations, analysis, and deductions past and future—is forcing one-sided performance, consuming valuable consultation time in orienting himself within the actual horoscope.

Sign and Ascendant Sign). The client will want to make some gracious small talk to release anxiety. This is normal. The consultation scene—the astrologer and the room—must give the client *positive* opportunities for reaction (compliments, registration of comfort, browsing for a moment among your books, etc.) rather than negative opportunities for criticizing (silently or overtly) dishevelment, interruption, uncomfortable surroundings, or anything that is not totally tailored to the time of sharing to come.

Second, what about your person-to-person relationship with the client: are you much younger or much older? Are you man to man, woman to woman, woman to man, man to woman, adult to child?

The consideration of age is very important: generational dimensions are immediately keyed; potential personal biases are illuminated. The young astrologer will have to work very hard to offset the psychological and sociological profile of the young when working earnestly with a client much older. The older astrologer will have to work very hard not to fit a generational mold that is instinctively expected by a much younger client. When astrologer and client are in the same age group, these tensions are not present, but the responsibility is great for the astrologer—in all cases, but particularly in the case of the same age group—to remain objective, to avoid over-identification with judgments and reactions that might be too easily shared.

There is the consideration of personal attraction between client and astrologer, between astrologer and client. It is not to be denied; it is registered almost immediately in many cases. An instant dislike for a client is probably mutual, and it is for the *astrologer* to eliminate this normal subjectivity from his or her awareness. An instant attraction to the client is probably mutual, and it is for the astrologer to view this as a bonus for trust and ease in communication, but to avoid having the comfort of the situation break down objectivity by inviting easy identification.

Again, the astrologer must know his or her self thoroughly. Knowing as well the direction of the consultation *beforehand* will help very much to keep subjectivity to a minimum. The best way to control an initially positive feeling is to minimize your reactions, knowing that the client is undoubtedly as comfortable as you are and being happy that the consultation will begin openly, easily.

If you are much shorter than the client, you will need to capitalize on an inner professional strength and poise to balance the client's instinctive awareness of the fact and perhaps the feeling of dominance or momentary withdrawal of respect. If you are much taller than the client, the caution is not to threaten by standing too close, to accept the instinctively felt respect from an intermediate distance: not too close to threaten, not too far to make sharing difficult.

Voice modulation is also important: most clients with a problem of introversion will speak very softly and will be threatened if your voice is very loud.

All of these considerations are very important to

establish a base upon which the consultation will begin. Adjustment of the sound of the voice, changing physical closeness, converting dislike into appreciation, comfort into self-motivating tension, will all occur in the consultation through the dynamic interchange between client and astrologer, but they must begin upon a base that gives the client maximum security and comfort.

Third, the astrologer should shake hands with the client. So often this is ignored in modern life, yet it is very important. The astrologer can feel the coldness or warmth of the hand, begin to perceive the strength or weakness of the client's self-presentation. Conversely, the client can begin to perceive the strength, calm, and comfort of the astrologer. All of these subtle observations take place almost immediately, during the greeting and courteous welcome into the astrologer's home-office.

Fourth, through the client's initial self-presentation, the astrologer can begin to perceive the strength of the Ascendant as a projection of the Sun-Moon blend. The body type is evaluated in terms of the Ascendant and the condition of the ruling planet (see "Rectification," Volume VII, page 225). Based upon the valid assumption that the client will want to present his or her best self to the astrologer, will dress and behave in the best way, the evaluation of the Ascendant factors, when matched with actual presence, is very rewarding.

Through consultation experience, you will have learned that there is something about you or your consultation room that will invariably attract comment from the client as the client hurriedly inspects the surroundings. Perhaps it is a particular painting or print on your wall; perhaps it is something about you personally, like your voice or your hair; your home itself; your desk, your sofa; the view out your window; anything that is in high focus within the surroundings. Learn to watch for this reaction; it is an important key to the projection of the client.

For example, it seems that a heavy emphasis of the eastern hemisphere (Volume IV), suggesting ego-absorption, will often correspond to the client who does *not* comment upon the highly commentable. The client tends to feel that giving a compliment is somehow diminishing. The self-absorption is intense. There are other concomitants as well: perhaps the self-absorption is from a structure of arrogance (Leo, Aries; powerful Mars structures) or depression (Saturn in the Ascendant and strongly configurated; northern hemisphere emphasis; retrogradation patterns, etc.) or simply from a personality formation that is remote, locked away, habitually recessive (Sun and/or Moon within the VIIIth or XIIth). There are many potential corroborations, different in every horoscope, but the relative balance of these configurations can immediately become obvious as the client fulfills the natural expectations of the meeting with the astrologer: an extension of his or her self.

If there is no comment forthcoming in reaction to what is usually commented upon by clients, simply point out the observation, try to stimulate a reaction: "Isn't this painting beautiful? It's my favorite; I bought it when I was in Florida, etc." You will be asking for a reaction, *inviting* the client to share with you. Deductions from the responses will be most rewarding.

There has been a strong interchange already, within perhaps the first two minutes that you are together with your client. The astrologer's perception must quickly begin to corroborate deductions in prepared analysis with behavior and response in actual presence. During these initial exchanges, the Ascendant and House positions of the Sun-Moon blend can be easily stimulated and evaluated; an inquiry about the job (if it is not the major consideration of the consultation to follow) can corroborate the Moon House position further (Volume IX), as well as the oriental planet, the Xth and VIth Houses; the value of the clothing, jewelry, accessories can corroborate IInd and VIIIth House configurations, certain aspect groups involving Venus, for example; awareness of your home and its appointments, IVth House and Cancer configurations; of your books, Mercury, Virgo, Gemini; spontaneous questions about Astrology in general, Aquarius; the level of enthusiasm, Jupiter; sexual empathy, the sex profile prepared beforehand (Volume IX).

Fifth, during the initial chatting, deductions can be made about education as well. Along with other observations, the educational profile begins to establish *level* within life experience, and our instinctive, learned, and studied awareness of sociology is alerted. Perhaps the client makes errors in grammar, an indication often that the education was interrupted (ruler of the IXth in developmental tension through aspects). We know sociologically that a person's speech stratifies him. Vocabulary choice will fill out these observations and clearly assist the astrologer in preparing the level of communication possible in the ensuing dialogue.

There is the consideration of race. A black astrologer must be as aware as a white astrologer that, although in principle racial tensions are being resolved sociologically, there still remain for the astrologer and client of both races inherited biases, learned reactions, and a past life of particular stress and personal concern. As individuals, the astrologer and the client share these areas of concern, and they must be consciously evaluated and adjusted within the consultation relationship to ensure maximum sharing.

Sixth, deductions about the nervous system can be corroborated quickly as well. Perhaps the client shows evidence of nailbiting, corresponding to a particular Mercury configuration with Mars or Uranus, to Gemini or Virgo. Other factors to consider are the speed of speech, the continuity of sentences, and the development of thoughts. For the astrologer to sense that he or she may never get a chance to say something becomes an important consideration that must be dealt with quickly. Perhaps the nervous profile is linked with introversion factors, suggesting a deep worry and anxiety.

Often, a client with a retrograde Saturn or a strong debilitation of ego references (the Ascendant, the IInd House) or relationship strengths (VIIth House) will close the eyes, sometimes with a rapid flutter, whenever saying something in the first person singular or offering some opinion or definite statement about the self. This is often a strong sign of inferiority feelings. The momentary closing or fluttering of the eyelids is like a veil protecting the weak self-concept, as if the person were listening to an inner voice of calculated superiority feeling that works to defend the weakness (Volume IV, page 38).

The client whose eye contact seems distant, dreamy, once-removed, often has the Mercury-Neptune opposition or square in the chart, suggesting day-dreaming and fantasy.

Body language becomes very telling, throughout the interview, but especially when the client is first seated. When the arms are crossed across the chest, there is definitely a registration of defensiveness or self-containment, often corresponding to a Grand Trine, especially in the Air Family. The body circuit appears closed. The astrologer should make a suggestion to open the circuit, to separate the arms and keep them free on the arms of the chair. (When the arm-cross is accompanied by tight crossing of the legs as well, the defensive posture is extreme.)

Watch for the rate and depth of the client's breathing; if quick and shallow, appearing to catch in the throat, making sentences short and gulped, the sound of the voice small and fragile, the client is extremely anxious about what's ahead. Simply asking the client to change posture or to exhale invariably brings a great smile, a humorous self-awareness, great relaxation, and establishes a rapport of understanding immediately between the client and the astrologer.

Seventh, a perfect way to begin conversation with the client after the initial moments of meeting is simply to ask, "How did you get my name?" Now, perhaps this was told to you on the telephone when the appointment was made, but asking the question again gives the client an opportunity to respond to you in terms entirely his own. The client can speak authoritatively, conclusively, and often complimentarily to the astrologer. Tension is resolved. A third-party endorsement makes both client and astrologer happy. Reputation is clarified in many ways. The client ususally brings himself "up to date," up to the moment: ". . . and that's why I'm here."

By this time, the client is seated with the astrologer in comfort. The astrologer has corroborated many of the deductions that had been made beforehand. The level is established. The relative balance of horoscope factors is much clearer.

What is most important is that the astrologer has not been *thinking about himself, about herself.* The astrologer is not preparing for a one-sided performance, but is doing everything possible to relate the client to the horoscope, to relate the astrologer to the client. All thoughts are directed toward the client, all reactions are shared with the client in human terms. The astrologer is not performing alone. He is preparing to share.

The best way to understand the implications of all of these observations is to study yourself: how do you project your own horoscope when you are in a new, challenging situation. For example, when you go to establish credit at a store, make an expensive purchase, attend a dinner party with new acquaintances, register a complaint with some service, talk with people from different strata of society, how do you behave in terms of your horoscope? What of you is projected when, how, and why? In such circumstances, you are behaving instinctively, either offensively or defensively. You are aware of which end of the matter you are controlling. You are making a presentation or receiving one. You are under scrutiny yourself. Others are sizing you up. Throughout any situation, you are working *to establish relationship.* Two "horoscopes" are meeting. The same dynamic is present in high focus between astrologer and client, between client and astrologer.

The emphasis upon relationship, upon perceptive service, eliminates the one-sidedness of performance. It opens the way to creative communication, illuminated analysis, and the learning and enrichment of both parties.

In this way, we trust our skills. Technique has been practiced and internalized, has become instinct. Just as an opera singer learns to trust his instrument as soon as the music begins, to be a vehicle between composer and audience, so the astrologer learns to trust his identity, to put the ego out of the way and become a medium of sharing. Indeed, he must be continually aware of the strategy of perception and communication, and this awareness encourages definite dimensions of theatricality in that behavior will differ with every client. But theatricality is resourcefulness in doing the job. Professionalism is this talent put to work upon demand. Service is professional adjustment to the performance demands of each situation.

We have come full circle: one-sided performing astrologically is "original sin," yet astrological counseling is performance! There is a difference: the nuance between performance of what we know (one-sided) and the performance in service to another of what is *relevant, helpful, personalized.* Performance is sinful in the prima donna, the one who is obviously isolated among others. It is graceful in the highly skilled and resourceful professional who can adapt to exigencies of all kinds, who can save the day.

We are one-sided performers when we feel for a moment that the planets *do* things, that such-and-such means this-and-that unalterably. We are one-sided performers when we fit others' lives to our own personal, rigid conception of analysis and counseling.

We are artists in performance when we recognize flexibility and versatility in our professional techniques; when we search for nuance, enrich deductions through learning, and relate them to the continually different needs of our clients. Then, we are performing our skill in service to man, not to ourselves, not to what we glory in knowing, nor to Astrology.

Communication

"Madame, you have a maxillary sinus discharge into the pharyngal alimentary canal near the esophagus, with acute inflammation of the epiglottis, especially when you are supine." This statement simply means that the client has nasal drip.

The same confusion all too easily exists through the use of astrological jargon: "You have a Grand Trine in Water, discharged by a T Cross keyed to Saturn, ruler of the VIIth, placed in the XIth House, disposed of by Mercury retrograde in the Vth." This statement certainly could describe a great difficulty in establishing successful love relationships, but the jargon would say absolutely nothing to someone not sophisticated in Astrology.

But how often do we use jargon when we talk to clients or to the public in speeches, newspaper interviews, radio or television appearances. Too often. The jargon means nothing. It only establishes *separation* of the astrologer, makes him or her inscrutable, esoteric, not "with it." Jargon is a symptom of the original sin of one-sided performance. It indicates that the astrologer has not seen the other side, the relationship factors that must be based upon sensitive, natural, helpful communication. Jargon must be translated into behavioral terminology—not as cause and effect, but as correspondence—to inform, clarify, and guide the consultation.

There is a very easy way to cover the symbology of the horoscope drawing quickly at the very beginning of the consultation. I personally feel that it is extremely important that the astrologer present the client with a clean, beautiful drawing of his or her horoscope at the beginning of the interview. The horoscope drawing is a kind of gift from the astrologer to the client. It establishes a strong sense of exchange. The astrologer has the horoscope working drawing for the consultation and for file records and reference in the future; the client has an objective picture of all that is to be discussed, to keep forever.

Upon presentation of the horoscope, the astrologer can place it before the client like this: "Mrs. Andrews, this is a copy of your horoscope. I have a copy as well, with lots of notes on it, as you can see. [This suggests to the client all the work you have done beforehand.] Here is what the astrologer does: he places the planets in their exact positions throughout the vault of the heavens at the moment you were born, from the vantage point of where you were born. [Pause, as the client looks at all the symbols in the diagram.] You recognize some of these symbols, I'm sure: [pointing them out] here is the Sun, the Moon, Mars and Venus, etc. The astrologer measures the angles between these planets, among several groups of them, for example like the relationship here [point to a clear conjunction or opposition]. We say that these planets are in conjunction [or opposition]; they are very close to one another in symbolic focus. We translate this kind of geometry into character traits, needs, experience, behavior

"Now, perhaps you're wondering why all these planets are grouped together in this area [if such a formation is clearly obvious], why this section is empty. Well, this is the astrologer's job. All these things mean something that is within your identity, your experiences, and your development."

That's that. You have explained what the astrologer does, indicated the extent of the work involved, and established your skill with an easy-to-understand technical summary, your organization and precision with a neat horoscope portrait that now belongs to the client. No more technical discussion is necessary. You are free to begin behavioral discussion with the client in the client's terminology.

By this time, perhaps no more than four or five minutes have elapsed since the client walked through the door. The welcome, the orientation, and introduction to the interview have been accomplished smoothly, naturally, professionally. The client has had a chance to adjust to the surroundings and to the astrologer. The astrologer has had many opportunities to observe the client, to match perceptions to the horoscope deductions already prepared. A balance has been revealed within the astrologer's awareness of the horoscope. Perhaps the nervous measurements are very pronounced within the client; therefore they will have more strength in the overall analysis. Perhaps introversion measurements don't appear as predominantly as had been expected; perhaps the client has outgrown them or learned to overcome them through another portion of the horoscope that speaks more strongly symbolically since the client's presence and behavior have shown this portion forthrightly. Body movements, sentence structure, clothing, speech patterns, personal rapport, all have been measured. The astrologer is more than ready to make an opening statement. Adjustments are incorporated. The introductory statement must hit home!

Old texts suggest a ring-around-the-rosy technique of communicating the horoscope: you begin with Sun Sign, then the Moon, the Ascendant. Then, one goes around the Houses, talking about money, brothers and sisters or communication and travel, the home, the parents, the love life, the work situation, etc. Again, the obvious one-sided performance dominates and, by such routine attention to the parts, the strength of the whole is unrecognized.

All work done throughout these volumes has been based upon a law of naturalness: relating the Sun-Moon blend (Volume III) to the identity, knowing that the significance of this blend must flow throughout the whole personality, throughout all the symbolism. Of course, the Sun-Moon blend will be modified by the Ascendant and, especially, by the aspects made by the Sun and Moon with other planets. In my opinion, the best beginning to analysis is an introductory statement that can flow very easily from the horoscope orientation given to the client. We want to capture the whole person, not a specific part. We want immediately to capsulize the identity to separate the client from all other individuals, to show that Astrology can capture the essence of a person quickly and accurately, and most important, to establish a concise base upon which the rest of the analysis of the horoscope will be built, a base that will be easily remembered throughout the whole consultation and after the client leaves.

The Sun-Moon blend is the basic component of this first statement. With the modification suggested by the

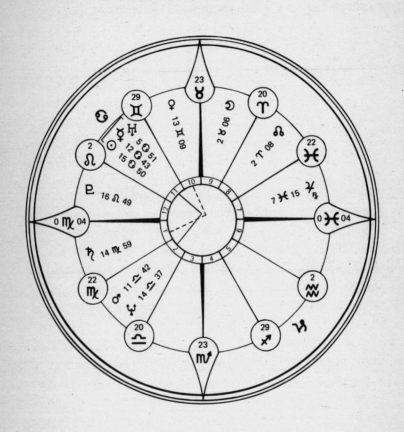

aspects, a short statement can be made extremely effectively. For example, the young man whose horoscope appears on page 22 shows the Sun in Cancer and the Moon in Taurus: we could expect graciousness, sensitivity; clarity of the self's purposes and gentleness of action in achieving them. There could be some kind of "magic" about the personal ability, an unruffled show (Volume III). But the Sun is square Mars, ruler of IX: there would be a tension suggesting interruption of the education necessary for the personality's organization (Moon in IX in Taurus) of potentials. His "ammunition" would be limited. The Sun squares Neptune: tension from a protective fantasy used to save personal self-esteem, perhaps through underachievement. The Moon is applying to a square with Pluto in XII: the personality might have organized many fanciful, high-minded opinions, probably based upon a keen hypercritical projection (Mercury Ascendant), might have had difficulty expressing these things fully and easily (interrupted education), and then felt that the world simply didn't understand him (Pluto in XII).

Mercury is square Mars and Neptune: further corroboration that there is a nervous preoccupation, a tension through fantasy. Mercury rules Gemini on XI and Virgo on II, the two houses involved within the square aspects: all the tension is involved with self-worth (II) and attracting friendships. Venus, dispositor of Mars and Neptune and ruler of the Midheaven, is square Saturn, suggesting an emotional confinement in reactions (Mutable Signs), very important at the core of the personality (Ascendant and Midheaven). Venus is trine Neptune, keeping the fantasy as it is, supporting it, making the self easy to delude (Mercury square Neptune) about self-esteem (II, X). This is reinforced by Mercury as dispositor of Venus, ruler of the Ascendant, and dispositor of Saturn.

Jupiter is retrograde in VII, ruled by Neptune, suggesting the withdrawal of enthusiasm from relationships. There is a strong reaction focus upon the eastern hemisphere, the ego.

The Venus square with Saturn will key discussion of the parental ·factors (Venus rules Taurus on X; Saturn symbolizes the father; and Pluto, ruler of Scorpio on IV, is squared by the Moon).

At first glance, there is an obvious anxiety over self-worth that will diffuse the Sun-Moon blend of life-energy. The core blend will have to be adjusted.

"Eric" arrived punctually. He was short, with small features (Virgo Ascendant), but there was an ample breadth to his appearance (Mercury in Cancer) that made him appear larger than he was. He was twenty-four, dressed in casual clothes with no real color emphasis. He said he was working as a janitor at a local college.

He obviously had had a long struggle with acne; his face was strongly blemished. This was strong corroboration of the Venus square with Saturn in particular and, secondarily, of the aspects among Mercury, Uranus, and Mars suggesting nervousness. I then noticed that he had a harelip, very unobtrusive and probably surgically corrected.

He was gentle, relaxed, and gracious to a fault. He

was casual, friendly, said the "right" things easily, and we quickly began to get into the interview. As I explained what an astrologer does, just as is outlined above on page 19, I began to adjust the basic general statement about the Sun-Moon blend I had prepared. I worked quickly in my mind to see this young man with his particular energies within society, with friends (strong XIth House), yet having problems with relationships, possibly keyed to parental difficulties, his nervousness about these problems contributing to the acne and the anxiety over self-esteem. I began to sense his graciousness as a *tactic to gain personal acceptance.*

"Now, perhaps you're wondering why all these planets seem grouped above this line here; the line is the horizon line in Astrology. Or perhaps why this area is empty. All these things mean something that is within your identity, your experience, and your development.

"Basically, we should begin with a general statement to differentiate you from the person walking in front of the house there right now or the next person you'll meet, all other people. The horoscope shows that you are gracious, friendly, that you express yourself softly, and that you're very sensitive. But, Eric, there are tensions here—there have to be in order for us to grow—and these are linked to self-esteem, how you feel about yourself. The horoscope suggests that, on the one hand, you're pretty particular about whom you relate to. This might be a defense because you're not too pleased with yourself. And, then on the other hand, you're friendly to the extreme in order to be accepted. Do you think that is accurate?"

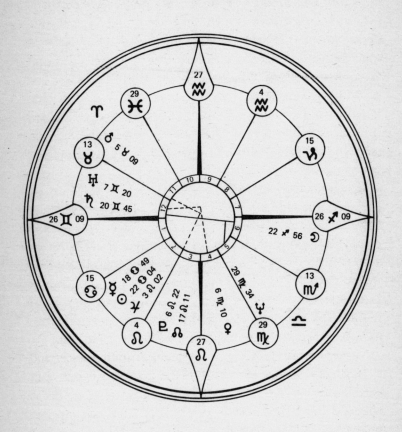

"Yeah (smiling). That's it, right on the button. Gee, I know a little about Astrology; how do you see all that?"

We talked together about a few of the technical measurements, and then went deeply into the life development: the anxieties about being loved, his constant questioning of others' responses to him. The major point of consultation was established when we both understood perfectly various pressures in his life (mainly parental) and how the self-deluding fantasy protection that developed (Sun-Mercury square Mars-Neptune) was supported too well (Venus trine to Neptune) and, as a result, tended to confine emotional expression, repressing it further (Venus square Saturn).

The analysis proceeded beautifully through the whole life (Volume VIII), and a base of self-confidence and practical participation in relationships was established to project him securely into new development in the near future. The consultation occurred when transiting Saturn was upon his Sun as Jupiter was transiting its own natal position: he had just made plans to re-enter college (after having left when Saturn had transited his Moon in IX).

The horoscope on page 26 shows a Sun in Cancer and a Moon in Sagittarius. This blend would suggest that idealism would lift the emotions, that high goals would be set, and that the beautiful, the aesthetic, ethical, and philosophical would have great appeal to the woman. Her plans for personal security would be long-range and very important to her.

The Moon is strongly aspected with Saturn. This would add a strong dimension of ambition to the overall need for security, perhaps to the point of self-limitation (XIIth). The Moon is square to Neptune, ruler of XI (love-received): a fantasy dimension would be involved with the grand elevation of the need for security, perhaps even deception or subterfuge.

Mars rules Aries in XI, love received, and Mars is square to Jupiter, ruler of the VIIth: here is a tremendous, demanding, stubborn dimension that perhaps will correspond to possessiveness in a relationship that fits her ideals for personal security. There probably has already been one marriage and divorce (Jupiter rules VII; the woman was thirty-one at the time of the consultation). The Mars square with Pluto is also indicative of disruption and rebellion, strong opinionation. Overall, the woman will demand what she believes is essential for her highly developed need for security: Mercury ties everything together as ruler of the Ascendant, dispositor of Uranus and Saturn, Venus and Neptune, aspected only in a conjunction with the Sun.

"Bettie" missed her appointment, telephoned the same day, and said that she had thought it was for the next day (Gemini Ascendant; perhaps it wasn't comfortable, "ideal" for her to come on the day agreed upon). She arrived the next day, twenty minutes late. She was slightly taller than average, very slender, very attractive. She was dressed in black and brown (Saturn rising in Mercury's Sign). She was very poised. She offered a few excuses for her lateness, and settled into a chair, completely open and relaxed. She said that she knew a good deal about

Astrology, produced her own horoscope drawing and that
of a man in her life. I placed the male's horoscope aside for
later and began the introductory statement.

"Bettie, the horoscope shows a tremendous idealism
that helps you set very high goals for yourself, for your
personal security. Have you ever been married?"

"Yes. I'm divorced now."

"And you don't want to make any more mistakes in
marriage, do you?"

She smiled simply.

"Well, as I look at you in your calm, your poise, it's
hard for me to say what the horoscope definitely shows;
you're really tenacious about fulfilling a relationship that
will suit your ideals. Perhaps it has to do with the man
whose horoscope you've brought with you, but there's no
doubt about it, you're almost shrewish in fulfilling your
needs for security. I don't see it in you, but I see it in your
horoscope. Is that accurate?"

Bettie agreed, with a little surprise. I suggested that
we should discuss why the need was so great and perhaps
how we could temper the tenaciousness and make life
more productive for her in her quest. The major point of
our discussion began with her relationship to her parents
(Moon opposed by Saturn; Uranus square Venus in the
IVth).

Her parents had broken up when Saturn had crossed
her Ascendant before her first birthday. She went to live
with grandparents, was caught between homes, then she
was taken in by her mother and a stepfather. Homelife was

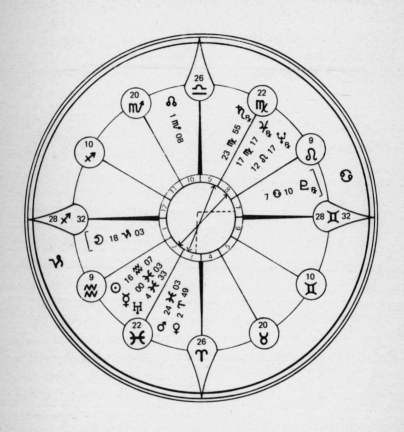

very hectic. Questions about her health profile (Volume IX), analyzing the tension aspects throughout the horoscope anatomically, revealed the strength of these tensions within the relationship and security crises: throat problems (Venus and Taurus), a heart murmur (Leo tension focus), colitis and an ovarian cyst (Virgo, Pluto tension constructs), problems in the lumbar region (Saturn; Venus as ruler of Libra).

These two sketches show the swift entrance into full analysis through a basic statement of the whole horoscope. The client is immediately involved in a reaction to the major statement. The astrologer is ready to seize points, reactions, words, additions of any kind, to develop the awareness of the whole even further.

The third example, on page 30, shows an extreme pull-back into powerful ego awareness (Capricorn Moon in I): Saturn, Jupiter, Neptune, and Pluto are all retrograde and are the only bodies outside of the northeast quadrant. The oppositions tying these groups together (Saturn-Mars; Sun-Neptune) suggest tremendous vacillation within the life. The only point of true developmental tension, the only square within the horoscope, is between Venus, ruler of the Vth and the Midheaven, and Pluto in VII, ruler of the XIth. In reaction to my careful statements and questions, the female client (age fifty-three) made the following comments. These comments alone can guide any open-minded astrologer through the horoscope and into full understanding, in a way that would be impossible without participation with the client:

- Indecisiveness? Wow! I can't even decide on the menu.
- My father was very much in the background.
- My life is so dumb. People don't accept me.
- I wanted more education, and this dominates my life still.
- Yes, I've lived my whole life through my only daughter.
- I used to have difficulty sexually. After all, I had twelve pregnancies and only one child! Nine miscarriages and two deaths upon Caesarian birth.
- Yes, then I wanted to commit suicide [progressed Sun square Pluto; transiting Saturn-Mars square Mercury-Uranus; Neptune square Mercury; Uranus square Moon]. I even told the priest that it wouldn't be a sin, because I was so unhappy.
- I feel unworthy of such a good husband. I don't think I'm a good wife sexually.

Detailed analysis showed this woman equating sex with having a baby, mainly through her dominating mother (Venus in Aries square Pluto) and the Catholic Church. She did finally have a baby girl. The daughter applied to a convent when her mother's progressed Sun opposed Saturn and conjoined Mars, a time when she would hope to see her own ambition fulfilled through her daughter. But this hope would have been torn apart (the opposition), and it was: the mother communicated secretly with the convent, damaging her own daughter's chances in order to keep her for herself. Her rationale was

"I wouldn't let God take this child too!" (Neptune opposed Sun; the VIIIth is the child's fourth; Sun in II, self-worth).

The daughter finally married and the woman's own mother died as Saturn transited the fourth cusp and the progressed Moon crossed the Midheaven. Three years later, the woman tried to commit suicide, her daughter and her reason for living gone.

At the time of consultation, the progressed Moon had just crossed her Ascendant and Jupiter was transiting her Sun: "I've been feeling better about myself lately."

The problem remained focused upon her relationship with her husband, still focused on the Venus-Pluto square, love given and received. Removal of the guilt about her intrusion into her daughter's convent application, improving sexual perspective despite the bad memories of difficulties with conception, formulating new plans with her husband, understanding his feelings throughout their life together became the main points with which to conclude the interview.

No one-sided performance of aspect delineation could possibly have captured the essence of this complicated individual. Within ten minutes of artful dialogue, through listening carefully to clues of all kinds to corroborate the behavioral manifestation of deduced synthesis, a richly textured life was revealed. A recitation of aspect meanings would only have eliminated the richness that came from creative communication and would have barely gotten below the surface.

The woman was helped considerably by Astrology.

She did more than her share to make the consultation profitable as a learning experience . . . and perhaps that is as it should be.

2

Objectification

Men are disturbed not by things, but
by the views which they take of them.
Epictetus

Many clients who have undergone various degrees of
psychotherapy have remarked after an hour or so of
astrological analysis, "It's amazing how fast you can
discover these things. It took months for my doctor to get
at the same information!" This observation highlights
perhaps the most important asset of astrological service:
the process of objectification. With the introduction of the
horoscope drawing, the entire identity of the client is
externalized very quickly, put on the desk top, becoming
remarkably free from personal censorship, defense
mechanisms, value judgment.

The Horoscope
Discussion of a powerful configuration associated
with disruption, if the psychological forces it represents
are not marshalled economically within behavior, is made

35

easy by reference to the drawing rather than to the individual: "I don't see it in you, but I see it in your horoscope." Often, clients will be amazed that an event or a character profile is revealed within the drawing. They will even lean forward themselves to inspect the picture they don't understand. Objectification helps them to avoid embarrassment, guilt, and intimidation.

Objectification mitigates the astrologer's subjectivity also. Discussions about incidents are framed symbolically within the drawing, within the astrologer's mind, preventing judgmental reactions. The astrologer is preoccupied with enrichment of the symbolic signals, linking the client's revelations to the astrological organization. The direct line to the astrologer's subjective self is detoured through the client's horoscope. The horoscope, embodying the disciplines of Astrology, helps the astrologer maintain professional, objective poise. The formal psychotherapist has various projective techniques (e.g., Rorschach and Thematic Apperception Test) as objectification aids when needed, but the astrologer has the horoscope drawing as an essential, a *sine qua non*.

The Companion Diagram

Using the great strength of objectification, the astrologer can dramatically clarify complicated astrological configurations for the client—still without using jargon. For example, the Grand Trine involves a minimum of three planets, three Signs, and three Houses. Additionally, there may be a conjunction at one or more of the points of the triangle; there are dispositor dynamics, rulership networks;

there are aspects made to points of the triangle by other planets, involving their rulerships, House references, etc. The pattern easily takes in a great deal of the whole horoscope, the whole identity. A separate diagram can objectify this major construct vividly.

The horoscope shown on page 38 has a Water Grand Trine involving Jupiter, Uranus, and Mercury-Pluto-Sun. Saturn squares the Sun, Pluto, and Mercury within the Grand Trine; Neptune is square with Jupiter within the Grand Trine.

With the Sun and Moon both in Cancer, we can expect a core energy within the identity that is sensitive and self-protecting. The home will be the castle. Emotions will be the shelter against the intrusion of the world. Affections and values will be sought within the security of the home. Loneliness can be accepted easily to avoid hurt by the world. This Sun-Moon blend is made quite serious through the square with Saturn. Since Saturn rules VI, we can expect a limitation within the identity's quest for security (XIIth), perhaps even sickness that confines her to her home, or a difficulty through the husband (Saturn is co-ruler of VII); at best, a tense withdrawal into the home and a very private contentment with loneliness. With Neptune rising and receiving an applying square from Jupiter in Scorpio within the Grand Trine, we can anticipate that much of the loneliness taken on within the self, within the home, will be rationalized through religion or things spiritual, psychic (Neptune and Jupiter are co-rulers of the IXth). The whole structure of the home situation is in extreme focus: the Sun, ruler of the

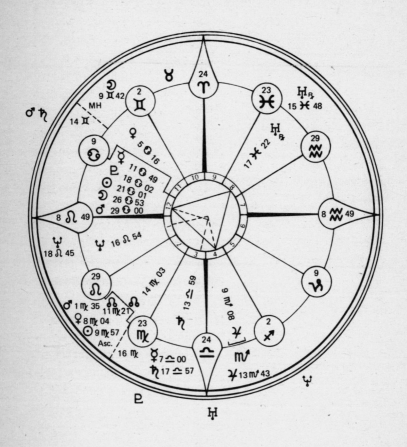

Ascendant, is in Cancer in the XIIth; Jupiter in the Grand Trine is in the IVth, the home; Jupiter and Uranus, the only bodies in the western hemisphere, are channeled into the Cancer stellium through the Grand Trine.

Roberta looked like a showgirl. At fifty-one, she was overly made-up, wore much jewelry, had a deep tan out of season. She had a regal bearing. The Leo Ascendant was very obvious. She wore dark blue clothing, keying the strength of Neptune rising and the Water Grand Trine.

Dialogue at the beginning of the interview disclosed that she stayed in and about her home almost exclusively, that she was very spiritual and practiced psychic healing within her home. She had been ideally married, and her husband had died suddenly five years before. In her conversation about the period when transiting Saturn conjoined her Sun in late 1945, early 1946, she said, "That's when my husband returned to me from the war." The "to me" part of the statement was odd, but certainly corroborated the ego emphasis within the home, the all-pervasive awareness of emotional self-protection and security.

All developments in the life were at the levels of redecorating the home and finding a metaphysical philosophy of life with her husband. I commented, "You're really the queen of your own castle, aren't you?" She replied, "Yes, I've always felt that the best things in life are for me."

At the time of consultation, the progressed Sun and Venus were sextile the natal Jupiter, ruler of the Vth. Transiting Uranus (ruler of VII) was crossing the fourth cusp, and transiting Saturn (co-ruler of the VIIth) would conjoin the Sun for the second time in her life in the summer of 1975. Roberta was surely having a romance. She corroborated this.

But progressed Saturn was very close to exact square with the natal Pluto, ruler of Scorpio in IV. It was clear that this second major romance of her life would make different demands upon her all-important home perspective. It would be vitally important for Roberta to understand that she might have to make an adjustment of her intense self-absorption in order to respect the identity of the man she was hoping to marry. To explain the Grand Trine construct clearly was essential. (In the quotation that follows, analytical commentary, added later, is put in brackets.)

"Roberta, this romance certainly seems like a good one. But, we've already seen together how fortunate you were in your first marriage to have such an attentive, dedicated husband. The horoscope shows exactly what you've indicated: that he doted upon you, returned to you after the war, grew together with you in your metaphysical explorations. In fact, he was the best thing in life for you. But now, as a mature adult, you are meeting another experienced adult, one who has set a life style of his own. There are some compromises you may have to make in order to make this relationship as fine as it can be.

"Look here: your horoscope shows a powerful closed circuit. It's like a three-sided billiard table: the ball goes from one corner to the next, then to the next, and back again.

Let's call this first corner [Mercury, Pluto, Sun] your ego, your self, everything you need in your life: love, security, a beautiful and comfortable home. You think about it all the time. You rule the roost [Mars in Cancer]; you're queen of the castle, as we already said. They're probably so intense in you, all these needs for love and security, because of early feelings about your father and his death [progressed Sun conjunct Mars, ruler of X; transiting Saturn opposed the stellium from its natal square with the Sun], or because of some karmic compensation [XIIth House]. I really don't think the reasons are important any more, but the needs are firmly established and have dominated your adult life.

"Okay. Now, the needs become organized through your enthusiasms, specifically through your religious and metaphysical sensitivities. All opportunities (at point E) are organized around fulfillment of the strong personal needs at point G [Jupiter in Scorpio in IV]—'G' for 'gains', let's say.

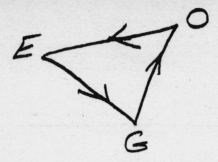

Then, other peoples' resources are involved to fulfill your individuality [Uranus in VIII]. Let's label this corner point 'O' for 'others'. When this takes place, the whole emotional need-circuit triumphs and it is very self-contained. The energies come bouncing back to a new level of the same needs, to point 'E', and the whole circuit of behavior begins again, and again, and again. Pretty soon there's a strong groove worn in the playing surface, a habit of expectancy is developed."

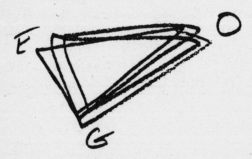

Roberta began to smile and laugh. She understood it perfectly and had noticed that the points spelled "EGO." "That will just help you remember it!", I said.

"Now, Roberta, this circuit is tied in beautifully to your love and affections [Uranus ruling VII; Jupiter ruling V; Mercury ruling XI] and to your work in healing and teaching crippled children how to swim [the Saturn-ambition developmental square into the Grand Trine as ruler of VI and co-ruler of the VIIth; the Neptune square with Jupiter], but in this next marriage, there are indications that much of this will have to change, that your new romance will ask you to alter the circuit, drop some of the ego, gain a new perspective in a new life. Do you think you're ready to do it?"

Roberta and I were talking about a problem that was on the desk, on a separate piece of paper. She could see it all objectively. As we talked further, she saw how well the circuit had worked for her, building enormous security and happiness in her life. She saw how she had very little to worry about any more. She saw the adventure of opening the circuit to an adventure at another level, with someone else, with different energies.

The consultation concluded humorously in recognition of how very much she needed someone else's help to do anything since she was so "charmingly impractical" (zero in Earth count).

Client Reactions

Using the horoscope and perhaps a companion diagram as a method of objectification, to get analysis outside of the client, can sometimes be supplemented with a subject-reaction technique: after the basic analytical statement has been made, the astrologer may continue, ". . . and the horoscope diagram suggests that there are several important points we will have to discuss. For example, your parents, your relationships sexually, your job dissatisfaction . . . all of these things seem related together. . . ." During this statement, the astrologer watches for the slightest reaction from the client, spacing the topic references carefully to allow recognition and response to each by the client. The astrologer *knows* these are important concerns, that they *are* interrelated symbolically by aspects and rulerships within the horoscope. He can learn from the client's slightest reaction (eyes, posture, mouth, words) where the strongest place to begin is.

I have had occasions when, at the mere mention of the father, a poised female client has spontaneously broken into tears, when clients have "tightened" up with the mention of sexual or relationship concerns. The goal of this approach is to help gauge the client's sensitivity to subjects so as to determine the level of tension and the objectification technique that will permit freest discussion.

With experience and well-developed perceptual skills, the astrologer can become extremely sure of a deduction through observation of the client's subtle reactions, even though the client is extremely defensive—even to the point of lying. Countless times in consultation, usually in the early stages, in reaction to a careful statement like, ". . . and how do these tensions we're discussing affect the relationship with your husband (or wife)?", clients have shifted their bodies into a defensive position, crossing arms and legs, closing their eyes for a moment, and said, "Oh, not at all. Everything is fine there." Reading the reactions in such a case is extremely important, especially if the astrologer is trying to corroborate a powerful configuration like the progressed Sun squaring Uranus, ruler of the VIIth, with transiting Saturn crossing the fourth or seventh cusp, perhaps involving Jupiter in a legalistic sense, etc. The reply then must be swift and authoritative: "The horoscope suggests that is not true. You're probably here really to get at this tension with your husband. Please, let's talk about it together. The horoscope suggests that your husband is not very enthusiastic about this project of yours, etc. [retrograde Jupiter in VII, for example], or that he is not as attentive to your needs now [Saturn in XI, his fifth], etc." Objectification is forced and is invariably successful.

What is accomplished by objectification is that events, "things," are separated from reactions, from "views." An event is placed, as it were, on a shelf. It is packaged, evaluated, and put away—not hidden from view, but placed out of reach, freeing the identity for other pursuits.

So-What-If Technique

Reactions are usually in the form of anxiety, nervousness, fear. That is, an outcome anticipated as negative is feared before the fact; an outcome experienced as negative is remembered after the fact, both to the point of debilitation. These anxiety structures are revealed in speech: "I'm worried about the child custody trial; I can't sleep, can't do anything. What if I don't get the rights I should have?"

In this case, the astrologer can look ahead and, within the whole-life structure already studied in depth throughout the consultation, pretty well determine the outcome of the trial (See "Gretchen's" case, Volume VIII, page 80). The objectification technique here is very simple: suggest the addition of the word "so" before "what if?" *"So, what if* you do lose, what then? Will life really stop for you, or is perhaps time trying to tell you something?"

Blow-up Technique

Another extremely good technique in dealing with anxiety reaction in anticipation or in hindsight is called the "blow-up" technique: in dialogue, the astrologer asks the client to blow up the anxiety description totally out of proportion, to exaggerate and flood the conversation with descriptions of the worst possible outcomes. Very soon after the fantasy narrative begins, the point of absurdity is reached. The astrologer should be all-smiles, encouraging the client to blow the concerns sky-high, even helping in the process. This objectification releases a great deal of pent-up exaggerated tension, establishes a real perspective through contrast with the absurd. Immediately, commonsense thinking stabilizes the situation and the client sees better how things really are.

But it is imperative to caution here that the astrologer must know *beforehand* upon what the anxiety situation is based. In anxiety over relationships (VIIth House), the base is probably linked by aspects and rulership patterns from the VIIth to the parental axis (X-IV), to the self-esteem points (II, X), to the love axis (V-XI). The double-rulerships by each of the inner-will planets (Mercury, Venus, and Mars; along with the Sun and Moon) will invariably be involved within the link-ups between problem area and problem cause, as well as the evaluation of behavioral, willful response. The final perspective of the blown-up anxiety situation is established by the anchor elsewhere, with the parents, with self-esteem, with love given and received. In turn, these base concerns will have ancillary reference to job, sickness, income, children. Often, the base of tensions will be between levels of meaning within the same house: IInd, self-esteem, self-worth and money, possessions; Vth, love given, children, speculation; VIth, sickness or job atmosphere; XIth, spouse's affections, personal friends, goals; IXth, education, spouse's travel, his or her communication; XIIth, limitation through the spouse's sickness, work habits, son or daughter-in-law's financial problems (the second of the XIth, which is the seventh of the Vth); etc.

The example shown on page 48 is a case where the anxiety tension was already so great at the time of consultation that hospitalization and psychiatric care were essential. The woman herself had exaggerated, blown-up her anxieties to such a degree that they imbalanced her whole identity. With the Sun in Virgo and the Moon in Cancer, we could expect that the life-energy flow would be built upon a kind of shyness within a highly specified and conventional code of behavior. The need for security

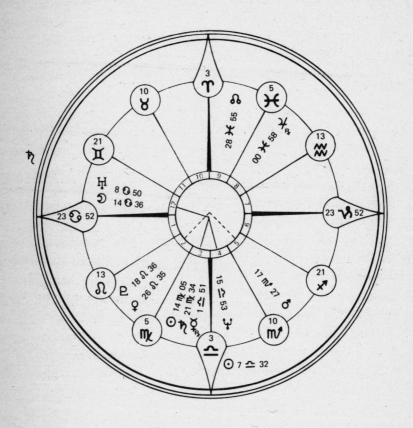

would gain intensity. Self-justification would become an art form. This Sun-Moon blend (from Volume III) is focused even more severely through the Sun's applying conjunction to Saturn. The ambition would take on all sorts of drudgery and detail to prove a point in service of the individual's needs for security.

The introversion dimensions were very strong: the Moon in XII with Uranus, Jupiter retrograde, everything else below the horizon. The mental profile was intensely defined: Sun, Saturn, and retrograde Mercury within III, Mercury square Uranus in XII; Neptune, ruler of IX, is the only planet in an Angle and is square the Moon and Uranus in XII; Mercury retrograde rules the IIIrd and the XIIth and is semi-square Pluto. Mars in Scorpio is semi-square Mercury and square Pluto, its dispositor.

This woman arrived for consultation shortly before her twenty-fourth birthday. She was extremely stout (the aspects to the Moon, ruler of the Cancer Ascendant), suggesting a corroboration of the intense, introverted mental self-indulgence to achieve security-need fulfillment. She said she was a microbiologist researcher, corroborating the powerful Mars, ruler of X, within the research sign Scorpio; and the Virgo dimensions. Vocationally, with Venus oriental (Volume IX), she would identify herself—her complex and tense needs for success, recognition, and security—with her work. Self-justification would be obsessively pursued to fulfill her ambition. It would dominate the perspective of her work-life: Venus in conjunction with Pluto in II, opposing Jupiter, ruler of VI, semi-square Uranus in XII and Neptune in IV.

As I observed her, sitting as comfortably as her weight would allow her, I noted that the pupils of her eyes were extremely dilated. I asked her if she were under drugs of any kind, and she said that she was sedated and that she was on leave from a psychiatric hospital to see me. Of course, this adjusted the level of the prepared deductions considerably.

At the time of consultation, the progressed Sun was applying to the square with Uranus, which would correspond to a tremendous nervous tension and anxiety about self-worth (Sun rules II), her mental reactions to the level of her ambition's fulfillment (natal Sun in III in conjunction with Saturn). Additionally, transiting Saturn was exactly conjunct Uranus in XII. She obviously was experiencing an intense break-up with all ambition and security goals she had set in her life. She took it personally and perhaps was even suicidal (Volumes V, IX).

"Well, Mrs. Rowan, I know you've worked hard, perhaps obsessively, to build a reputation in your work, and perhaps you've sacrificed an enormous amount to justify all your effort: your figure, your health, perhaps even your family. If you are married, have been married, even that is surely breaking up under the strain now."

"You're right. I've just gotten a divorce this month, and I admitted myself to the hospital for help."

The woman had had a brilliant, precocious career as a microbiologist. She revealed how she had worked day and night, sacrificing friends, family, health incredibly, demanding isolation, yet support, from her colleagues.

When I asked her what her goal was, she calmly said, "I wanted to with the Nobel Prize before I was twenty-one."

The obsession was definite. Her vocabulary and clarity of thought were superb. There was an extraordinary intellect at work, which wasn't easily seen in the horoscope.

I asked why she was in the hospital. Was the reason suicidal thoughts? She replied that she had taken to burning herself, her arms and thighs, whenever anxiety had built up to an intolerable level; anxiety about getting the work done, fulfilling her goals and needs, gaining justification for the work that identified her. She showed me huge scar craters on her body, described pounding her head into walls, watching match flames incinerate her flesh, pressing up against others' lit cigarettes in crowded streets or on buses. She told a harrowing story calmly. The blown-up exaggeration of the identity's needs was formidable.

There was nothing for Astrology to do. Indeed, it was relatively clear when the tension of time would diminish, but that was some time off. She had to go through much adjustment of life-goals in the meantime. We began to talk at a very sophisticated level about the meaning of work, the projection of self through work in service to the world, the orientation of self to goals established for identity.

Gradually, we both began to see the exaggeration a little humorously. Mrs. Rowan participated easily with many descriptions of the obsessive work compulsion. She had isolated herself from friends within her lost perspective of self-worth (Venus, ruler of Taurus on XI, conjunct Pluto, square Mars, opposing Jupiter, semi-square Uranus and Neptune).

I asked her if she had any friends, and she replied, "Only my parents, my child, and my husband, whom I'm still very close to, but I knew he was suffering from my behavior." I asked if she had ever taken time off for her child or to make other friends, to establish a normalcy in cooperation with reality. She said no.

I quickly diverted the discussion with the following question, perhaps the ultimate blow-up exaggeration of her work compulsion: "Mrs. Rowan, how long did it take God to create the universe?"

"Seven days," she replied emphatically.

"No, you're wrong. He worked for *six* days, and rested on the seventh."

This was a dramatic moment. She and I just sat quietly. She understood, exhaled fully, smiled, and, after a moment said, "You're so right. I see the point. But, you know, the doctors at the hospital aren't talking to me like that at all."

"Well, why don't you think about this some more and talk to *them* this way?"

For the conclusion of our time together, we discussed the point we had established in practical terms, studied a projection of her time of tension through the next two years, and ended remarkably refreshed after what had been an extremely demanding hour.

There was no real cause for her aberrance. Somehow, through some reasoning process, her interpretation of things, of events, her views had blown out of proportion and disturbed her behavioral balance. Perhaps it was meant to be, to establish a perspective for the rest of her life through which her own genius will serve the world more strongly.

There is a very fine line here between what level of anxiety an astrologer can learn to handle on the spot with different techniques and what level of anxiety he must refer on to specialists in chemo- or shock-therapy, in deep guidance therapy over an extended period of time. On the one hand, the astrologer's own perspectives within the world must determine the value of a commonsense approach, i. e., the blow-up technique for example or just rational reasoning, in relation to the client's capacity to see those fresh perspectives easily; on the other hand, the astrologer must be able to see that the time of tension may be so extended, the focus of anxiety so great and thorough that only extended, specialized care will be helpful *during the time period astrologically determinable*. Specialized therapy will rarely speed up the process that can be measured astrologically, but the client will be made more comfortable during the period by people and techniques dedicated to this kind of care.

Other Objectification Techniques

Rarely does an astrologer meet with clients in such severe distress. Most often, anxiety, worry, fear are manifested with reactions that respond well to new perspective through common sense, through humorous exaggeration, through the objectification techniques of

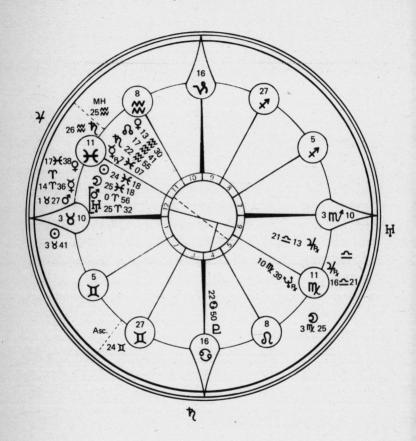

imagery and parable. "Normal," non-chronic anxiety is usually alleviated by improving the perspective on the problem, by finding the real cause. The client's recognition of the new perspective, seeing it objectively, does wonders.

Imagery

Anxiety, worry, concern are often focused *in time* as well as upon subjective reactions to an event. Through the technique of imagery, the astrologer can help the client project ahead in time, away from the moment of riveted anxiety focus. The male's horoscope on page 54 shows a New-Moon birth in Pisces: the life-energy will be ultra-sensitive, perhaps diluted into a listlessness of reaction, even an indecisiveness (New Moon, Mutable Sign, XIIth House). He will probably gain much through support from partners, from his wife (Sun-Moon trine Pluto, ruler of VII in IV). But, at the same time, a partner or his wife may *control* any individual response potential he has: the only developmental tensions within the horoscope (squares) are within the T Cross Uranus-Jupiter and Pluto. Pluto is the only planet in an Angle.

The man will resent this strongly (Mars in Aries in XII) and will try to buck the organization of this other person in order to achieve his own organization (Taurus Ascendant). But he is really caught in a bind through the T Cross and the opposition of Mercury retrograde and Neptune retrograde in Mutable Signs. The Mercury-Neptune axis falls in the Vth-XIth love axis; Uranus rules Aquarius on XI (love received) and is within the T Cross; Saturn is in the XIth gaining conjunction through Venus' application. The focus must primarily be upon a domineering wife.

At the time of the consultation, the progressed Sun was conjunct the Ascendant, the progressed Midheaven and Saturn were in conjunction in the XIth, sextile natal Uranus; progressed Venus was sextile the natal Midheaven; transiting Saturn was two months away from the fourth cusp, and transiting Uranus was opposing its own position and nearing the seventh cusp. The man was being reborn. A whole new self was in formation, an entire new being that would affect his home (fourth cusp), his marriage (seventh cusp), and his whole self-projection (Ascendant; Sun ruling V), through his job as well (Midheaven measurements).

"George" made a fine appearance: strong, friendly, handsome. His speech showed surely that his education had been interrupted (Jupiter, ruler of IX, within the dominating T Cross). He spoke easily and uninhibitedly, but was constantly analyzing his feelings, apologizing for opinions. When it came to volition, will, opinion, he was like a marshmallow. He had had a succession of sales jobs and was momentarily unemployed, in between an old life and the new life that was surely to come (progressions and transits).

The consultation flowed smoothly throughout all the important transit and progression development points in his past life. He had a choice of several job possibilities. The horoscope helped make the choice as a behind-the-scenes (Moon in XIIth) trainer of sales personnel. He would make his income in such a sales training position through a percentage split with the front-line salesmen he trained. (Mercury, selling, rules II, income, III, selling, and VI, co-workers, and is in awareness opposition with Neptune, both retrograde, suggesting a dimension of once-removal, kickbacks; Neptune rules Pisces on XII, business partners' work activity, disposing of the Sun and Moon. Mercury and Neptune are in mutual reception.)

After all of this was fully established, the new life was deduced and then corroborated by the base established in the past forty years. At this point it was necessary to discuss his relationship with his wife: "George, this is all fine now. We know where you are going, what you will be able to do best, but we've got to discuss your wife's reactions, how they can inhibit you through over-control, and actually affect your job performance [discharge of the T Cross into the Xth]."

"Aw, gee, she's always after me to get more money. Why she even keeps a separate account of her own job money, and always bugs me to get her cigarettes and stuff outta my money. I said to her, 'Why the hell are you doin' this? . . .' " He went on and on about the domineering nature of his wife over the years.

"When *was* your wife happy with what you were doing on the job? Was it that time you were selling insurance and won that big reward for excellence, that long trip?"

"Yeah! That was probably the last time."

"That was in March, 1963. We determined that earlier when we were discussing your past."

The reward had come to him exactly with the Jupiter transit of his Sun and Moon. The month before, in February of 1963, Saturn had transited Venus: ". . . and just before your reward, were you really at odds with your wife then? Was she all upset with your work?"

"Yeah! Always the same."

"And then, bang, you got the reward, the trip, and everything was okay?"

"That's the way it always is."

"And what's going to happen now . . . now that you have this big chance to make an important shift professionally, really to be yourself, to get out from under finally? What's she going to do? Will she be helpful to you?"

"Not on your life. She's a real bitch. I don't know what I'm gonna do."

George was clearly completely dominated by his wife. They had not had any love relationship for months. They were crucially at odds, all based upon his supposed inadequacy in providing well enough for her and their children. The wife herself worked but contributed nothing to the family security. George slumped; he couldn't imagine himself making the break to a new job, a new level of self-expression. It would mean leaving his wife and children, requiring strong will and self-confidence. We both knew this; his situation at home was simply intolerable.

His anxiety was riveted to the depressing status quo. I tried to get him to imagine himself in a future time: "George I was able to pinpoint that rewarding time for you eleven years ago in March of 1963, right to the month, because of an astrological measurement. Everything we've talked about has been extremenly accurate. What if I tell you that the same reward pattern is going to repeat itself early in 1975, in February to be exact [transit Jupiter conjunct Sun and Moon]? Doesn't that give you something to look forward to?"

"You really think so? Really? But I can't believe it, there are so many problems now . . ."

"You mean there are many things you have to do in the in-between time?"

"I guess so."

"Look, imagine yourself a year from now. Say you divorce your wife as you have so often thought of doing, wished you could do. Say you get this job training the salesmen. Project your income for me. They've already told you what the job potential is. Just imagine right now that you're free and have worked hard for a year, and it's reward time in February. What will it be like?"

George then took paper and pencil, computed a tidy income based upon hard work, salesmen's returns. He projected himself into sexual freedom, greater esteem in new friendships, pride on the job, success.

"Wow! Looks good doesn't it, George?"

"Yeah, it really does, but . . ."

"DO IT!"

George's anxiety had lost its hold upon the status quo. He had objectified and seen himself at a future time. The imagery established a new view of the situation, and my abrupt and firm command-suggestion stabilized it. We then talked about a schedule of getting a lawyer, providing for the children, taking care of domestic problems, about strategy on the job, what the independence would mean in terms of enjoyment but also in terms of responsibilities. George was off and running with new hope.

He got the job, began very successfully, and has moved out from his "wife's home." He made the decision when we had anticipated, on 16 September 1974, when the New-Moon transit occurred in opposition to his Sun and Moon and sextile his Pluto. Saturn was precisely upon his fourth cusp, Uranus precisely opposed its own natal position, Mars precisely opposed its natal position. The progressed Moon (ruler of IV) was precisely conjunct Neptune as well. (George's father died at the same time as this major life shift was initiated.)

Parables

Making a point by telling a story is an essential technique in the teaching process. Using a parable objectifies a predicament and allows a comparison to be made. The goal of all counseling is to provide to the client a clearer perspective, a more outspoken and less inhibited self-confidence. Clients after successful counsel usually express a more dominant attitude: they are able to offer opinions without fear, establish relationships without feeling inferior, take control of situations, plan ahead, forget problems. An invigorating kind of aggression is born (Mars, applied energy) that is the same thing as the will to live discussed in Volume IX. Parables can show stories of triumph over adversity, solution within perplexity, resolution after tension. The client will identify with the person and situation in the parable.

The parables can be stories from the astrologer's own personal life: surmounting illness, changing professions, "making things happen" through plan and preparation. They can be from the astrologer's other cases; from history; science; from the theatre, from fiction, famous peoples' lives, etc. Even memorable quotes from the famous supply strong parable emphasis. For example, to enlarge a perspective shrunk by inferiority feelings, Eleanor Roosevelt's statement is very effective: "Remember, no one can make you feel inferior without your consent." Walter Lippman's quote is very helpful in interpersonal relationship tensions: "To understand is not only to pardon, but in the end to love." Bernard Baruch's statement, "We can't cross a bridge until we come to it; but I always like to lay down a pontoon ahead of time," is helpful in alerting a client to the importance of preparation for challenge and opportunity revealed through progressions and transits.

The Stop Technique

In the moments of consultation, the client experiencing tension feels completely isolated. Relationships have not helped to fulfill needs. Tension has mounted. The client's anxiety is momentarily all-consuming. The client feels sorry for himself, often to the extreme. Perhaps the martyr attitude has been a habit over many years. Perhaps the client even enjoys it for the attention it attracts. Every astrologer will meet the client who incessantly dwells on personal misfortune. The anxiety factors have swirled into a dissociated complex, cut off from the rest of reaction potentials. The thoughts go around and around and build up in intensity. A shock is sometimes needed to interrupt the process.

The astrologer in good rapport with the client and yet faced with a non-stop, self-pitying recitation of gloom, usually accompanied with statements like, "I'm sorry, I can't help it; I just can't stop thinking about it," should wait for just the right moment when the client is caught up within the rhythmic repetition, and shout "STOP!"—sharply, loudly, and forcefully, *with no movement of the body*, no aggression at all, except for the imperious command of the voice. The client will be stunned into silence.

Then, quite normally, the astrologer should continue *immediately*: "There, you see. The thoughts do stop. (Smile.) Now, let me tell you about a person who had a problem much like yours, but much more severe, I think. This woman . . ."

The parable gains admission into the consciousness of the client. The self-pitying or the anxious review of subjective reactions has been interrupted.

The effect is often so definite and, after the instructive parable, so rewarding, that relief of anxiety is extremely noticeable. The astrologer can even further suggest that the client practice this (with the astrologer and later on his or her own) *so that the client can mentally shout "Stop!" when the reactions begin again and bring*

*the anxiety complex to a lower intensity and eventually
eliminate it.*

Humor

Objectification is an extremely powerful tool. It is
one of the first steps to maturity (Volume V, page 144),
extension of self and objectivity. Humor almost invariably
accompanies self-objectification. If the client's sense of
humor about himself *cannot* be activated in the slightest, it
is a sign that the anxiety syndrome is very deep and
perhaps serious enough to require special diagnostic
techniques (Chapter IV) and/or specialized medical
assistance.

The concomitance of humor with self-
objectification became most clear to me some years
ago, when trying to stop our four-year-old daughter from
crying. She was old enough to have a self-concept
developed. She would be crying heavily, and I would pick
her up and put her face in front of a mirror. She would see
herself all tear-stained and twisted, and she would
suddenly stop and, after several different instances, she
would immediately begin to laugh at herself. Some years
later, I would simply have to say, go look at yourself in the
mirror, and the anxiety would diminish. But, when the
emotional pain was severe, when more then just the
self-concept was under tension, she would reject the mirror
game. Then, of course, the tension focus was quite serious,
requiring help.

So it is with adults. It's hard to be distraught in
public or when looking into a mirror. Seeing one's self as

others do, seeing "somebody else," is quite a sobering experience. This is the therapy accomplished through many, many techniques of objectification.

In Will Rogers' words, "Everything is funny as long as it is happening to somebody else."

3

Organization

Every astrologer—student or professional—constantly faces
the challenge of synthesis: organizing many measurements
into a representation of whole identity. The overall
geometry of horoscope composition (Volume IV) and the
law of naturalness based upon the Sun-Moon blend that we
have developed throughout these volumes help establish a
theme, a major current, a level of identity registration.
Within detailed synthesis, we have seen how we can take
segments of synthesis and relate them to one another,
causally, commonsensically, and supportively (Volumes
VIII and IX). We test these synthesis constructs
throughout the past in order to establish a reliable base for
projection into the future.

Now, face to face with the client, the demand for
organization is urgent. No "catalogue" of astrological
measurements will ever do justice to whole identity. We
must organize our deductions in terms of needs,
motivation, tension, and support factors. Within ten or
fifteen minutes we should be able to organize clearly the
whole configuration in personal, human, and experiential
terms.

Elements and Their Houses

Remembering the basis of Family and Mode organization within the zodiac and in relationship to the House structure of the horoscope helps us appreciate how much organization *has already been done by nature,* by the creative principle. It is there to guide us in sharing understanding of the identity naturally created. For example, the Ascendant, House V, and House IX are naturally linked by the Fire Trigon. There is supportive rapport among the measurements of ego projection, love given, and cooperation with the philosophies of the societies in which we live. The interrelationships of these three zones can be understood at other levels as well: the self is formulated at the Ascendant, is passed on to one's children (one's own facsimile) in the Vth, and blends directly from itself or through one's children with the communications of others in the IXth (the third of the VIIth). The fundamental ego speculates about its worth and uses the social mores to project. The cycle recycles itself at ever-changing levels of awareness, development, and projection.

The Earth Trigon links one's point of honor or professional position (the Xth, the Midheaven) with the base establishment of self-esteem, self-worth (the IInd) and the support of work relationships and service (the VIth). The optimum health profile within society through work and effort is seen within this practical circuit.

The Air Trigon links relationship dynamics (the VIIth) to friendships, love-received, social goals (the XIth), and the work of the day-to-day thinking, reacting, and communication processes (the IIIrd). On another level, this Trigon relates cooperation constructs (VII) to the assets of the professional position (XI, second of X), and potentials for social, professional, and educational mobility and change (III).

The Water Trigon indicates the rapport among the early home experiences (IV), the establishment of them within the organization and esteem profile of others (VIII), and the final assimilation of all experience (XII). This Trigon defines the emotional resources at work within the identity, the unconscious, the spirit, the feelings.

The delineations of these circuits are endless through creative House reading. Understanding the symbolic power of the Sun in the Xth must presume understanding the relationship between the Xth and the IInd, the Xth and the VIth, and then between the Xth and the other Houses, starting with the Xth as the new base in derivative House reading technique. If we see *only* the Xth in our understanding, and then only another unit, and then another, etc., we approach a drowning point, inundated by isolated specific measurements that defy coherent, natural synthesis.

Modes and Their Houses

Similarly, with the Modes, translated into experience potentials through the Signs' natural placements upon the horoscope, the behavioral hologram has many vital dimensions naturally: the ego projection will have to be aware of the need to relate (opposition, I-VII); the ego projection in development will naturally face tension with the positions of the parents (squares, I to X-IV). This Grand-Cross relationship within the Cardinal, Fixed, and Mutable Modes throughout the horoscope naturally organizes the developmental tension and awareness dimensions of life experience. The IInd House relates to the VIIIth by opposition, by awareness: self-worth and the worth of others; to the Vth and XIth as a dynamic experiential T Cross: self-worth profile in developmental tension with the love-given and love-received axis within personal experience.

Behavioral Cause and Effect

Indeed, these observations catalogically are obvious and simple, but in translation to behavioral tensions within experience the obvious becomes the basic. Isn't the way one thinks (III) necessarily matched with how one's society thinks (IX), and then isn't this mental-attitude profile, this communication potential, developed within the process of working, with co-workers, within service to others (VI), within the accumulated experiences of institutionalized life (XII)? Tensions within these obvious networks can become unbalanced to the point that relationships suffer, or the way one thinks is self-limiting or clashes with the behavioral expectations of others. *The obvious astrological network becomes the basic behavioral cause.*

Seeing the "plumbing" of the aspect patterns really allows Astrology to discuss cause and effect without inhibition: it is not the planets that cause effects, of course; it is man within experience who causes different levels of tension in order to allow growth. Man seeks to satisfy needs of all kinds. Needs cause things to happen.

This natural organization astrologically offers us an enormous vista of practical knowledge when we translate the description into behavioral understanding. All this is obvious to the utmost when, in the exposition paragraphs above, we convert the square (modal House relationship) into a trine (through an interception, for example) or the trine (elemental House relationship) into a square. Behavior expectation changes.

Rulerships

Another uncannily productive, natural organization aids the astrological analyst: the fact that the planets Mercury, Venus, Mars, Jupiter, and Saturn have dual rulerships of the Signs. This means that when we translate an astrological "plumbing" network of aspects into behavioral development within experience, *several Houses are interrelated within the developmental tensions* through tenancy, rulership, and dispositor dynamics. This means that several different zones of experience, of behavior, are related within the motivational causes of experience, activated by the individual to fulfill networks of needs. This is causation seen behavioristically, seen astrologically.

Perhaps the greatest single psychological contribution to organized behavioral insight is that what we are as adults is often profoundly attached to what our parents were to us in early life. Psychoanalysts refer to the birth trauma, and astrologers refer to the birth time. The whole of the maturation process of the individual is focused upon the relationship process, relating hemispheres of the horoscopes, fulfilling awareness axes of oppositions, building upon the developmental tensions of squares, maintaining the status quo through the support and ease of trines and sextiles. The need for relationship as the means to the end of individuation is the reigning need of the human.

Within a developmental aspect network, the chances are extraordinarily high that a VIIth House tension (relationship) will be related through rulership and dispositor dynamics to the X-IV axis, the parents, to the focus of self-worth (the IInd), to the ego projection (I), and/or to the V-IX axis, the love given and received. Seeing this natural organization behavioristically is the psychological way of modern Astrology.

To describe such an astrological network in *non-astrological terms* literally brings Astrology *to* Life. For example: a stellium of Mercury, Sun, Venus, Saturn, Jupiter, and Uranus in Fixed Taurus squared by Mars in Aquarius at the fourth cusp says just so much. The translation into behavior (horoscope shown on page 8, Volume V) says so much more: the native's mind, selfhood, aesthetics, ambition, enthusiasm, individuality and nervous system are under extreme developmental tension from within the home, probably from the father, focused problematically within the relationship process. With the Moon in Cancer in the VIIIth, this relationship tension is extremely debilitating because of the reigning need of the personality for security within the home, within emotions. Rulerships by Uranus and Saturn of the IVth, by the Sun of the Xth, introduce the parents crucially; placement of the Sun in the VIIth, ruled by Venus within the tension-wracked stellium, focuses the problem upon external relationships. The "gulf" of synthesis translated into living behavior *releases within the astrologer a vast amount of learned knowledge: from the behavioral description keyed by the astrological signals, the astrologer can anticipate how the native will react, how he will behave.* The horoscope drawing now lives within the individual; the deductions alert knowledge within the astrologer. Two humans relate for understanding.

With the problem areas acknowledged, the behavioral profile anticipated, artful dialogue and sensitive questioning can release corroboration of detail and nuance from the client. Then, progressions and transits noted throughout the past suggest to the astrologer the times when and how the problem areas were specifically excited (Mars), coalesced (Saturn), expanded or redeemed (Jupiter), intensified to the extreme (Uranus), perhaps camouflaged (Neptune), or given different perspective (Pluto). Again, Astrology keys the time and developmental dimensions, and the translation into behavior frees the astrologer's knowledge of life into a living portrait offered in service through self-understanding. The whole process affords rich self-acknowledgement through sensitive objectification. The search through the past (Volumes VI, VII, and VIII) reveals varying levels of reaction within client behavior. The astrologer stores these deductions in an accumulating awareness of the whole. The life is developed to the present and, beautifully, client and astrologer sit face to face in grand awareness of the whole, in humanistic terms. The step into the future is

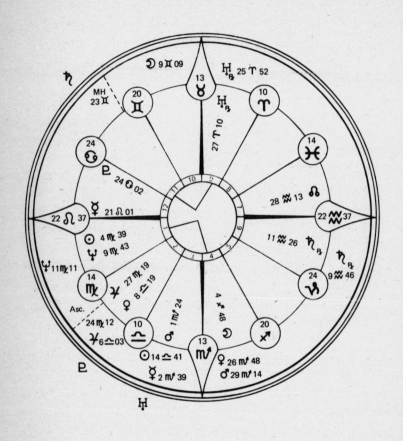

made together, easily, naturally.

A woman came to my door without an appointment last month. It was two months after her forty-first birthday. When I answered the door, she was still, almost in a trance. I identified myself, and she simply said, "I need your help."

I asked if she were in trouble. She said that her whole life was in trouble. She started to cry. The pupils of her eyes and her strange neurological calm suggested that she was under heavy medication, which she corroborated.

She was slender, with very small features, nicely dressed, pretty, extremely sad. I told her I had no time that day, and she replied, "But *this* is my time, " almost as if she sensed some kind of predestination in the moment of our meeting. I asked her to return in three hours, and I made a rearrangement of my schedule so that I could see her. I asked her if she were running away or if she thought of taking her life. She said yes to both questions. I told her that we would "live her life together" in three hours. Through this careful phrase, I tried to build hope within her, to relate her positively to help to come, to hold her in comfort in the intervening period.

Her horoscope showed problems that had started with her very birth, a very strong accentuation within the present (fall, 1974), and much improved prospects for the future.

The Birth Organization

The Sun and the Moon are in exact square, suggesting that her parents, her home, were in upheaval at the time of her birth. The blend of the Sun in Virgo and the Moon in Sagittarius suggests a mental tension at odds with things as they are. The mind will lead her into almost experimental opinionation and idealistic demand to develop her individuality. The tension factors in this blend and within the rest of the horoscope would take much practicality away from the process and substitute a fantasy, personal demand, an overdeveloped need.

The focus of the Sun within the Ascendant and ruling it is complicated by the conjunction with Neptune (also squaring the Moon). The mind in its fantasy demand, perhaps in defense against tensions arising at birth, is further accentuated by Mercury's position upon the Ascendant (Mercury is dispositor of the Sun, Neptune, and Jupiter).

The focus of the Moon within the IVth accentuates the home. Corroborations of early home difficulties are accumulating: Saturn retrograde in Aquarius suggests a legacy of inferiority feelings inherited from a father figure who perhaps was taken out of the picture early in life. Saturn gains a square development from Mars in ten years (Solar Arc). The accumulated tensions of the home would begin to project themselves within relationships (Saturn co-rules VII).

Uranus, ruler of the VIIth, is retrograde and square to Pluto, which, with Mars, rules Scorpio on the IVth, one of the parents. Mercury in XII is semi-square Venus, ruler of Taurus on X, the other parent. Neptune is exactly semi-square Pluto and is in conjunction with the Sun and square the Moon. Neptune rules half of the VIIth and the VIIIth, relationships and others' resources.

Because of heavy tensions in early life, within her home, the native works to find her own self-image through projections of idealistic, hypercritical fantasy. Perhaps this is complicated by a "princess complex" (the Leo Ascendant, Mercury tensions, Venus strength in Libra, trine Saturn), *a natural reaction*. Mercury rules Virgo on II, self-worth, and Gemini on XI, love received: the woman is very caught up with thinking about her personal value, her self-projection, in reaction to heavy memories of parental tensions in early childhood. She adopts an attitude of "the world simply doesn't understand me" (Pluto in XII, personal perspective under limitation and, here, in tension with Uranus in IX, society's ways, ruler of Aquarius on VII, relationships). Pluto's reference to the IVth through rulership is obvious.

Jupiter in II in Virgo suggests that her hope for reward will be in highly detailed terms; i.e., her fantasized self-ideal will demand exactness in order to vindicate her self-worth (Jupiter in II, other measurements) before she can give love (Jupiter rules V), fit in with others' constructs (Jupiter is co-ruler of Pisces on VIII), and all of this will naturally be sought in her home as a child (Jupiter is dispositor of the Moon within the tension constructs, placed in the IVth).

Her energy (Mars in Scorpio in III) can easily take "negative," i.e., debilitating forms: the pressure to run away from (III) imbalanced situations that she can not change her way (Libra on the IIIrd), rebellion against others' opinions (Mars rules Aries on IX and opposes Uranus which is square to Pluto). This is a very real developmental tension since Mars in progression will develop the square with Saturn, associated with threatened bad judgment. The focus is again upon the early beginnings, the family home, since Mars co-rules Scorpio on the IVth.

Basically, this is the birth synthesis. Although it requires some 500 words of description, it requires only perhaps sixty seconds to see by following the Sun-Moon blend tension throughout the aspect networks and rulership references, always seeking corroboration of the initial major deduction: trouble in the early home.

The questions that lead outline synthesis here, after the initial deduction, are as follows:

- How will the person react to early home difficulties? With the Sun-Moon blend basically mental, opinionated, and idealistic, and with this blend under strong developmental tension, there will be high expectancy, high need to adjust, to overcompensate within her own home relationships by seeking a highly prescribed ideal there. This self-projection will be difficult to externalize because of the inferiority feelings and the fantasy elements working defensively.

- Can we relate this growing deduction to the zones of home and relationship further? The rulers of the relationship zone and the home zone are under heavy tension to each other. Where these significators are located suggests further dimensions of the self-limiting reaction factors (Cadent House emphases within the horoscope).

- What about the self-image? The Ascendant and IInd House relationships with the other structures complement the deductions further.

These three questions naturally organize the behavioral whole, but then there are a few points that are still not easily explainable and which require more careful attention: though Venus is semi-square Mercury and rules part of the parental axis and the communication zone, it is trine Saturn. This would suggest that an inner superiority feeling compensates for the inferiority complex. In combination with the suspected "princess complex" and strong Ascendant, perhaps this works too well within the mental fantasy and prescriptions set up for love and relationship. Mercury is trine Uranus: a deduction similar to Venus-trine-Saturn is possible, since Mercury is upon the Ascendant, semi-square with Venus (which is sextile the Moon), and rules the XIth and IInd. Finally, there is an accentuation of the unconscious here (Volume V): the Water Signs upon the IVth, VIIIth, and XIIth Houses, their importance in the synthesis, and the prominence of their rulers and the trans-Saturnian planets. This tells us that within her unconscious, the tensions and debilitations of early home life work still with her tensions as an adult. She has not been able to shake them off, to displace them, to see them objectively.

Organization of the Past
We know that heavy transit or progression relationship in development within time affecting the Sun

and Moon (in square relationship at birth) will be very
important. Similarly, transits of the Ascendant (as well as
of the other Angles) will be important because of
Mercury's position there at birth. A most important time
will be at age eleven, when, by Solar Arc, Mars
symbolically progresses into a square with Saturn. The
booklet by Raphael, *Geocentric Longitudes and
Declinations of Neptune, Herschel, Saturn, Jupiter, & Mars:
1900 to 2001,* will provide the transit points at a glance,
and the Ephemeris will provide the important progressed
positions equally quickly. The whole pattern of
development will organize itself as delineated in the case
studies in Volume VIII of this series.

The major points of development in this case are as
follows:

T. ♄ ☍ ♀   Spring of 1938, age 5 years, 3 months: the
T. ♃ ♂ VII   home upset, father out of the picture,
T. ♅ ♂ MH   mother and daughter move.
T. ♇ □ ♅
(exact)
P. ☉ ♂ ♆

T. ♄ ♂ MH   Springs of 1940, 1941: other moves.
T. ♃ ♂ MH

T. ♄ ☍ ☽ □ ☉   Springs of 1942, 1943: mother's
T. ♅ □ ☉   alcoholism problematic; many stories about
S.A. ♂ □ ♄   these harrowing experiences.
('44)

T. ♄ ♂ ☌ ♇ October of 1945: daughter returning home to find the police trying to help the mother.

T. ♄ ♂ ☌ ☿ Asc. November of 1947: depression; sexual
T. ♅ □ ♃ awareness; no friends, reliance upon
T. ♆ ☌ ♀ fantasy life in aloneness.

T. ♄ ☌ ☉ ♅ Summer of 1949: problems continue: "Just awful, more of the same."

T. ♄ ☌ ♀ October of 1951; 1952-53: married to get
T. ♇ ☌ Asc. away from the horrible home situation; "I
P. ♂ ☌ IV knew it was wrong to marry as I did it."

T. ♄ □ ♄ November of 1954, all of 1955: separated
T. ♅ ☌ ♇ from husband, moved; on the job, she was
T. ♄ ☌ IV offered a promotion but she was "afraid to
P. ☉ ☌ ♃ take it."

T. ♄ ☌ ☽ □ ☉ July, November of 1956: good position
T. ♆ ☌ ♂ gained in work; 1957-58, with the Neptune
T. ♃ ☌ ☉ transit, the mother was ill and required hospitalization.

T. ♅ ☌ ☿ Asc. August of 1960 through spring of 1962: a
T. ♇ ☌ ☉ period of readjustment, new line of work,
T. ♄ ☌ ♄ working for a new image, a new
P. ☿ ☌ ♀ perspective.
P. ☉ into ♎

T. ♅ ♂ ☉ ♆
T. ♅ ♂ IV
T. ♄ ♂ ♂ VII

Fall of 1962 through summer of 1964: big romance.

T. ♄ ☍ ☉ ♆
☐ ☽

Mid 1964-early 1965: great frustration about being alone, insecurity feelings returning. Married in 1966 with progressed Mars square Mercury: "I knew again that time too that I shouldn't have done it."

P. ☉ ♂ ♀
T. ♃ ♂ ☉
T. ♅ ♂ ♃

Fall of 1967 through summer of 1968: a strong romantic affair, a seeking of improving self-worth and acceptance in relationship.

T. ♄ ♂ ♅ ☐ ♇

Spring of 1969: the build-up of this strong transit into the symbols of her tension problems broke down her stability to the point that she committed herself to a psychological clinic. No romance fulfilled her fantasy ideals. Her fantasy within self-projection was always frustrated. The wound of early homelife seemed so great as not to heal.

T. ♅ ♂ ♀

End of 1969 through 1971: another romantic adventure.

T. ♄ ♂ ☐ ☉,
☍ ☽

Again, her ego felt assailed with insecurities stemming from early life: in the spring of

T. ♅ ☌ ☽,   1972 she "ran away" from everything,
    □ ☉   roamed in search of a new beginning; she
P. ☽ ☌ MH   contemplated suicide.

P. ☽ △ ♄   August through October of 1974: again
    □ ♅   quit a good job and fled in depression.
from X

Organization of the Future

The years ahead appeared positive for her. Progressed Jupiter was applying to a conjunction with the natal Venus, and this fine conjunction would be in formation for the next eleven years! Progressed Venus would sextile natal Jupiter next year, in 1975. Progressed Saturn in retrograde would trine natal Venus for the rest of her life. These measurements promised romance, excellent work situations, and surely a long-awaited maturity (extension of self, self-objectification, unifying philosophy of life).

The tensions of the moment, suggested in progressed Mercury conjunct natal Mars, would soon disappear.

The progressed Moon would square Jupiter, trine Mars, and conjoin Pluto square to Uranus through the spring of 1978, marking a time when her past problems would again possibly affect her. Then the progressed Moon would go on to the Ascendant, its passage marking a developmental period of high challenge to her when opposing natal Saturn.

Transiting Uranus would cross Mars in December of 1974 and during all of 1975, corresponding to romance, but also to nervous anxiety.

Saturn in transit would conjoin Pluto and square Uranus in the summer of 1975 and cross her Ascendant in August of 1977 as Uranus crossed the IVth in November of 1977 and the middle of 1978 (with progressed Moon conjunct Pluto and square Uranus).

The life ahead had periods of tension, to be sure. But it promised a good job, a mature love relationship. Full understanding of the dynamics involved through the whole life would help her anticipate the periods of tension, see the supportive help within a mature romantic relationship and a good job. The counsel took the direction of understanding, anticipation, and the relaxation of fantasized ideals.

Most importantly, the native learned throughout the dialogue and objectification of her life problems to see how she was projecting her problems upon everyone around her, how she lost perspective in her personal life and her relationships through her fantasy of ideal expectation. By always seeing how forlorn she thought she was, she had lost sight of how valuable others were as individuals and as partners with her in her life. In our conversation, humor about herself was stimulated. A very simple adage seemed to focus all we talked about and helped her gain an external perspective (Pluto was to transit Venus in Libra): "It is more blessed to give than to receive."

Together, we learned to understand how nothing had ever been given to her throughout her whole life, and how she had never really given anything of herself to help make her dreams come true. I sent her home wreathed in smiles with the plan of daily making someone else happy and counting the rewards she gained from this prodecure. This would strengthen her self-perspective in relationships for the times of pressure to come. These potential problem periods would hopefully be understood as challenges rather than as continued victimization. Her real needs (Moon in Sagittarius) would mature from an anxious review of past life to a seasonal adventure of living to come.

This woman persisted and seemed to bloom into her new philosophy of life quickly: she got a fine job, became socially active, and sent me a very revealing thank-you card: "It's nice to know that you were there *when I needed you.*"

Plato observed: "God ever geometrizes." To understand, so must man. The architecture of any thing has an organization of its own. The way the parts of any whole hold together determines its life. The horoscope is a blueprint only. It has fantastically varied organizational potentials, but it does not have life. The human will is required to animate the celestial diagram and wind the cosmic clock. The meeting of client and horoscope brings Astrology to life.

The astrologer is the medium, the midwife who nurses sense and understanding into the networks of potential. Together, client and astrologer groom the revelation of life to corroboration and fulfillment.

In Bertrand Russell's words, "The only thing that will redeem mankind is cooperation."

4

Special Diagnostic Techniques

Well organized, perceptive, self-aware, the astrologer proceeds to analyze the horoscope with the client. Careful dialogue ferrets out corroboration of the major dimensions of synthesis. The networks of needs and the tension to fulfill them lace together areas of experience and levels of relationship. In nature's organization, the identity in its vast richness seems to revolve upon one or two major areas of need, meaning, and operation. Investigation of the past has uncovered routine reactions to challenging growth pressures. Ideals have met with fulfillment or frustration. Patterns of response have emerged. The present evolves within this continuum of habitual personality response. The future will take place within the maturing stream now known from the birth moment, seasoned through growth periods over the past years.

Objectification has helped enormously to portray the life of the client to the client. The exercise of memory to recall the important times of the past has taken the client's mind off his or her momentary point of tension and focused it on a whole developmental process. Mistakes and accomplishments have blended together to form a complex texture. A kind of balance emerges that becomes obvious.

But perhaps full recognition of the core tension still eludes both astrologer and client. Perhaps the astrologer, knowing the core problem (an anxiety over self-esteem, for example), has been unable to get the client to see it for himself, or the client refuses to agree that the situation is so, even though many events and reactions to them have made the premise clear.

There are several techniques that are very powerful in uncovering a core truth, that help to break through whatever concealment that still remains, whatever blind spot that has grown throughout years of oversight. These techniques further advance objectification.

Special note: These techniques are acutely personal and probing. The astrologer cannot possibly dare to use them unless his or her skill is seasoned with mature self-understanding, a proven ability to synthesize a horoscope analytically in depth, and a dedication to the sensitivities of each client. The astrologer must know what he is after in using these techniques; must know what to do with the answer when it is revealed.

The Desert Island Fantasy

A businessman came to me for consultation. He was extraordinarily successful at a very early age. He and his wife had an ideal family life and a new-born child. His concern was for important business decisions he knew he had to make in the near future.

In the process of our interview together, discussing

his extreme nervous energy as it related to his creativity, speculative interests, and sexual profile (Vth House: Venus square Mars in Scorpio; Mars semi-square Jupiter and trine Uranus, ruler of Aquarius on the Vth; Mercury rising in Libra square Uranus), we discussed his sexual relationship with his wife. The horoscope showed a difficulty here: Saturn and Pluto were conjunct in his XIth, his wife's Vth. Pluto was semi-square his Uranus in IX (his wife's communication IIIrd). His Moon in late Libra was conjunct his Scorpio Mars. The Moon ruled his Midheaven.

The revelation corroborated the aspects perfectly: he had a strong sex drive and need—as well as a strong need in financial speculation, business activity, etc., that had made him so precociously successful. His wife didn't seem to respond often enough or in the way that he wished. They had talked it through, but there was no improvement. He was not receiving enough of a sexual outlet at home. The frustration—the only frustration between him and his wife—kept his nerves high and threatened disruptive activities.

I checked the Ephemeris for his wife's birthday and noted that she was an Aries (also the Sign upon his seventh cusp) with the Moon in Gemini. He corroborated her personal power, her style of nervous expression and volubility. He remembered that she was born sometime after 9:00 P.M., which would put Scorpio on the Ascendant and Aries on her Vth. They were the same age: her Saturn would be conjunct Pluto as well. But most important here was recognition of the ego needs (Sun in Aries), the cerebration connected with their fulfillment

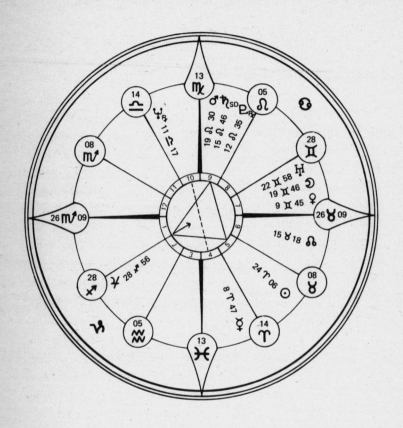

(Moon in Gemini), and the fact that Venus was in Gemini as well: "Camelot is better dreamed of than visited" (Volume III); her aesthetic awareness is lifted to the fantasy level. Mercury was clearly in Aries, probably near the fifth cusp, and was in close opposition with Neptune. This "daydreaming" fantasy axis would be a dominant dimension within her horoscope. Looking even more closely in the Ephemeris revealed that the Sun, Mars (ruling the Vth, inferred through mental approximation of the horoscope), and Jupiter would be in a Fire Grand Trine, suggesting further self-containment, surely involving the sex profile specifically. This, seen at a glance from the Ephemeris, was sufficient to begin to anticipate her problem: a fantasized, self-contained sex profile, somehow based on satisfying strong ego needs privately, not on seeking fulfillment in relationship with her husband. I suggested that his wife make an appointment as well.

"Mary" was twenty-six, on the short side, slightly plump, cheery, pretty, very well dressed, obviously precociously affluent, due to her husband's success.

Her horoscope (page 88), drawn for the exact birth time on her birth certificate, revealed many of the structures anticipated from the abbreviated sketch made from the Ephemeris and approximate birth time. The Mercury-Neptune fantasy axis dominated the horoscope. The self-containment of the Fire Grand Trine was made even stronger by Jupiter's opposition from within it to Uranus and the Moon in Gemini. The sexual profile registered "hot and cold" because Mars, ruler of V, was in conjunction with Saturn. This conjunction in the mental IXth again lifted the profile to the mental level. Pluto, ruler of the Scorpio Ascendant, was in the IXth as well, within the conjunction and retrograde. Mary had only the Midheaven in Earth and only the Ascendant in Water: the cerebration and motivational self-containment (Air and Fire) were extreme.

There was no square within the horoscope, no developmental tension to break up the self-containment. Only three oppositions focused the horoscope's awareness: the Mercury-Neptune axis dominated the chart; the oppositions of the Moon and Uranus were both made to Jupiter in Sagittarius, within the Grand Trine, ruling the House of its tenancy (along with Saturn), the IInd, the House of self-worth. Mary's self-image, perhaps her enthusiasm about sexual expression (trine Sun and Mars, references to the Vth), were self-contained, shaped by fantasy and mental awareness. Throughout the interview, very little revealed what might be the anxiety about self-worth, the reward from the fantasy that limited full sharing with her husband (Venus, ruler of Taurus, on VII, was trine Neptune; i.e., the fantasy kept the aesthetic relationship as it was, not open to change, fulfilled through the daydreaming). Venus was semi-square to the Sun in the Vth: she would know very well that this was a tension. She would be able to talk about it, but somehow not fully.

Throughout the consultation, many other points were covered about her need to be recognized, how that was achieved through her baby, how she viewed the big business plans her husband was making, etc.

When full rapport was established and Mary was very relaxed and appreciative of the insights accomplished through Astrology, I began to turn the converstaion to her sex profile.

"Mary, please, may we talk about sex for a moment. How often do you and your husband have intercourse?"

"Oh, not as often as he'd like, I know. I guess about two or three times a week, whatever's normal."

"I guess that is normal for most people, but you say not for your husband."

"Right. He's got a strong sex drive."

"Don't you?"

"Well, I don't know; it's never been a concern one way or the other. We're very happy together. It's just this point that we talk about sometimes."

"Of course, you're happy. Do you fantasize independently about sex?"

"Oh, only occasionally (a little surprised) . . . just occasionally."

"Would you mind telling me what your fantasies are when you do?" (Here trying to get into the cerebral self-containment)

(Rather embarrassed and hesitatingly) "Well, I guess I can tell you. I've told you everything else about my life. I see beautiful women in my imagination. Really beautiful bodies, like models or movie stars."

"Just women, never men or your husband?"

(Smiling, but quite embarrassed) "Yes, just women, really beautiful women."

"Well, of course, your horoscope says perfectly

clearly that you're not a lesbian (both of us laughed). Is it that you don't think you yourself are that pretty?"

"Oh no, I'm okay, a little chubby."

"Does your husband complain?"

"No, he really appreciates me."

"Well, why do you think you fantasize this way?"

"I don't know." (Mary began to withdraw. Her arms crossed each other upon her chest. The tone of her voice was final.)

"Look, Mary, please uncross your arms and make yourself comfortable. Let's have some fun with a fantasy. It's called the Desert Island Fantasy. Now, please know that I'm not stepping out of line here; I just want to see something. You'll enjoy this, and we'll learn something."

"Okay (much more relaxed)."

"Let's pretend that a magician is coming into the room. He has a magic wand and, 'bing,' with just a touch he is going to transport you to a desert island for six months. Time will stand still here; nobody will know you've been gone. All the necessary comforts will be on the island. Nothing to worry about—except maybe explaining a glorious tan when you get back! (both laugh) But the magician asks you to make a choice first: you can go alone or you can take me with you."

"I can go alone or only with you."

"Yes, that's the choice. If I had that choice, I'd certainly take you . . ."

"Well, I wouldn't go alone . . ."

"Right, neither would I. I'd want company."

"Okay, I'll go with you."

"Good. 'Bing'; we're there. It's a beautiful island. Really beautiful. What would be the first thing we'd do?"

"Oh, I guess we'd explore the island."

"Well, that would only take a few minutes. It's a very small island."

"Ummm, I guess we'd talk a lot together . . ."

"To get to know each other?"

"Sure. We'd have to learn a lot about each other . . ."

(The conversation becomes momentarily bogged down on this point of "getting to know each other"; the obvious is being evaded; other insignificant activities are observed.)

"Mary, don't you think we'd get around to having sex together?"

"Well, I don't know . . . uh . . . we could find lots of interesting things to talk about. You really have to know someone pretty well. Oh, I don't know."

"Now, let's be realistic. Don't you think, sooner or later, this would come up: we'd have sex together. After all, it's a beautiful island, nobody knows we're there, and it's pure fantasy?"

"All right. I guess so . . . it's reasonable . . . we probably would." (She said this with anxious reluctance; something inside her made her uncomfortable.)

"And, Mary, how would you feel afterwards?"

(A very long pause.)

". . . uh . . . (deep in thought) I'd feel I wasn't good enough . . . pretty enough . . . . Oh! THAT'S IT; I understand now (completely relaxed in recognition)."

"You do understand then. You feel unattractive,

unworthy. Yet you *are* attractive. You have everything anyone would ever want; at such a young age! And this is the make-up of your fantasies, isn't it?"

"Yes."

As the fantasy drama ended, Mary understood fully how inadequate she felt. The phrase for the Jupiter-Uranus opposition in Volume III is "wishes lose reference to reality." Because of the fantasy axis, the self-containment, the cerebration, the higher-mind perspectives, linked easily with the Vth, IXth, and IInd Houses in particular, it was no wonder that Mary could attain sexual fulfillment through her fantasy *alone*! In sexual relationships with her husband, she employed the same fantasies for fulfillment, completely independent of his expressivity and stimulation.

Counsel then worked to bring the two of them together, to enable the sharing of the fantasies during sex. We discussed techniques of communication that would open the fantasies and relate them to her husband, on the assumption that his reactions would mirror her worth as she was. The interview ended with many specific points about her husband's major business plans, reflected in her horoscope as well, about how she would fit into them, and how much more significant their togetherness would be in such times of change as their sexual relationship improved together. The time together in astrological counsel was extremely successful and very gratifying.

The Desert Island Fantasy removes the individual from his or her present moment in time. The environment is changed so that freedom to be is at a maximum.

The goal of the fantasy, though most often sexual, is not always so: the goal might be to reveal an authority problem within introversion. For example, since the astrologer represents an authority figure, a professional being paid for specialized services, a withdrawn, introverted client could be led through the dialogue into taking responsibilities on the island, cooking, caring for the dwelling, organizing entertainment. Anything at all can be built within the fantasy structure. If routine chores and concerns are not involved in the therapy, the "magician" can see to them all. If a challenge is needed to test the client's reactions, the magician can provide this situation as well.

Man and man: between the male astrologer and the male client, the fantasy premise is structured a little differently. If a concern with homosexuality is to be explored, the astrologer adapts his role accordingly; if it is an authority situation, two women are placed on the island waiting—i.e., the sex dimension is taken care of—and perhaps the authority situation will come down to the client's eventual jealousy that the astrologer's female companion enjoyed the astrologer more than his own companion enjoyed him. Perhaps the two men would have to struggle for a leadership position in the context of events or situations contrived by the magician upon the island, within the initial premise.

Woman and man: between the female astrologer and the male client, the fantasy proceeds similarly. Perhaps the premise must be structured to dramatize aggression, timidity, excellent performance without the intimidation of competition or being "found out." Another frequent situation would be the inability of the man to take charge of "things" on the island, when the female astrologer would carefully point out that she couldn't possibly manage alone. The premise is constructed to approximate the real-life problem bothering the client; the fantasy suspension allows the problem to be illuminated once-removed, as it were.

Woman and woman: between female astrologer and female client, the structure is similar to "man and man" above. If the client has a long history of tension with her mother, daughter, or sister, for example, the relationship can be structured to duplicate this real-life situation. Sex can be put out of the way by having two men already on the island; or the astrologer "stays behind," and the client meets a man on the island. Perhaps the problem is one of aggression and competition, with links to social self-esteem. If the concern is lesbianism, the astrologer must structure the premise along these lines to uncover the truth seen within the horoscope.

Age difference: if the astrologer and client differ considerably in age and the object of the fantasy is not a parental situation that would lend itself perfectly by virtue of the age difference and sexes of the client and astrologer, or *if the astrologer does not feel secure enough when personally involved within the fantasy projection-identification,* another person can be created to fit the role required and be awaiting the client, transported there in fantasy. Then, the astrologer simply supplies the conversation needed in dialogue through the third person, e.g., "He or she would certainly want to organize your life on the island ... or have sex with you ... or become jealous, etc."

A projection into the future is often a rewarding part of the fantasy. For example, "Now, considering we would have an ideal, complete relationship on the island, how would you feel when you returned?" Then, the next question: "What would have made the relationship ideal?" At all times, the astrologer, especially if participating, *can be* judgmental, since he or she is involved too, and it is all "only pretending." If the client gives a reaction that is impractical or is in the routine of real-life hedging, the astrologer should rationally challenge the reaction and, aided by the fantasy objectification, the client will usually be able easily to adjust the reaction to what is more natural, more normal, more cooperative—in the fantasy and in real life. The fantasy drama must behaviorally approach the realistic and the normal. In judging the scene, the astrologer leads the client to objective evaluation of behavior.

Clients will remember the rewards of the fantasy technique. The outcome will serve as strong reminder of the counsel situation.

Final note: if the client chooses to go to the island alone (very rare), the choice of solitude opens up exploration of the reasons for the choice. The client will say something like, "I'm such a bore, I wouldn't want to inflict myself on anybody else," or, "I'd like to be alone for a change without somebody always bugging me." After the attitudes are explored, the astrologer then can concoct a second attempt at the same fantasy, restructuring the premise to fit the attitudes under review and study. When solitude is chosen without flexibility at all, the inner personal fears are extremely strong and difficult to unlock. They are linked to extremely debilitated attitudes toward relationships. A second fantasy technique may be helpful: After the Holocaust.

After the Holocaust Fantasy

The astrologer describes the world devastated by some cataclysm. The astrologer and the client have been placed in leadership positions over the few remaining alive, with the responsibility to recreate laws, standards, mores, societal programs, codes of behavior and relationship. In other words, in fantasy they start life anew. Together they work out through discussion the ways people *should* behave. Of course, the client is projecting his or her own ideals, and the astrologer is matching each ideal with rational retort. It is a game of Devil's Advocate. The questions answered that have the highest value are those concerned with human dignity, human rights, cooperation, relationship, religion, the meaning of life.

The dramatic and typical outcome of an After the Holocaust Fantasy is given in Dr. Arnold A. Lazarus's superb book, *Behavior Therapy and Beyond* (1971,

McGraw-Hill, Inc., pages 175-176):

> Therapist: just tell me if your "Divine Force" will lay down rules about birth control, sexual intercourse, and dozens of petty "dos" and "don'ts" in all other areas of behavior?
>
> Patient: Oh, gosh! I don't know. I've never thought about it this way. I mean, suddenly you're asking me to examine and maybe revise my whole thinking.
>
> Therapist: That's exactly what I'm asking you to do.

With this point reached, the astrologer can enter into a discussion of all human values with the client, specifically directed back to significant events of development already established through the horoscope within the client's past life. The perspective is enriched by the client's major fresh contribution to his or her way of seeing life. The new value perspective is then projected into a behavioral and relationship plan in the future, in phase with the astrological date projections.

The Closed Circle Technique

This technique is very helpful in taking the interview to a deeper level of significance, especially when the conversation with the client remains superficial, trivial, uncooperative. Again, it is an objectification technique. It works to establish an operational trust between the client and the astrologer.

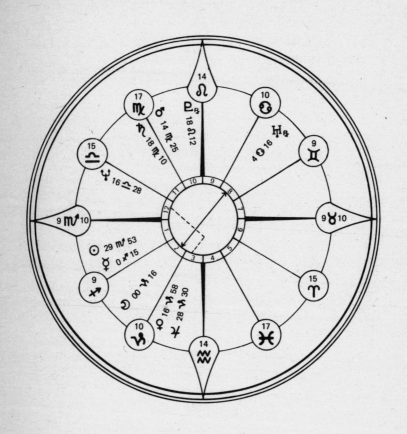

A stream of dialogue that is going nowhere, that is obviously skirting the core of an issue seen by the astrologer within the full synthesis of the horoscope, is interrupted by the astrologer, a drawing is made, and the client is asked to open the closed inner circle within himself, to share a secret that invariably focuses the remainder of the interview in depth and in productive sharing.

A female client with marital tensions obvious from the horoscope, yet revealing nothing in this regard at all during conversation, when taken into the closed circle of the diagram, stopped dead in conversation, paused, and blurted out—in relief—". . . something I've never told anyone else, ever? . . . I was out with another man last week."

Here is how the technique works: the horoscope shown on page 100 belongs to a strong, beautiful young woman, a medical doctor. A year after our initial consultation, she asked me to do an election chart (Volume VIII) for her forthcoming marriage at the end of June, 1975.

"Helen's" strengths are obvious: eastern hemisphere emphasis, Moon in Capricorn opposed Uranus; Sun rising in Scorpio; Fixed Signs on all the Angles; Mars in Virgo with Pluto in the Midheaven.

There were parental problems in her life (Moon opposed Uranus, ruler of IV; Sun, ruler of X, semi-square Neptune and quincunx Uranus). She has a tremendous need for love and respect (Saturn in Virgo in XI; Mercury, ruler of XI, conjunct the Sun; Saturn, co-ruler of IV and dispositor of Venus and the Moon). Venus makes the only significant developmental tension square within the horoscope, with Neptune in the XIIth, ruler of the Vth. Her emotional adventures have taken her through drugs, sexual experiences, and peculiar relationships. She "grew up" when Jupiter transited her Sun as Saturn applied to opposition with her Sun during the first six months of 1971. Now she was focused upon her medical work, was extremely settled and dedicated, anticipating an excellent marriage.

She plans to marry another doctor, who is in the same residency program at the same hospital as she is. They came to the marriage-plan interview together. He was equally energetic, recently divorced, seemingly mature and dedicated in his description of their jobs together and their plans for their marriage. Yet, he had several little nervous movements that betrayed an uneasiness. Even after lots of sharing and humor in the discussion of the marriage date and time choice, the subtle nervousness continued. She, in contrast, was totally calm, determined, clear, filled with self-conviction.

"Greg, would you mind giving me a moment alone with Helen? You can wait in the next room there. She'll share what we talk about with you later, but it will be easier for us to cover several points if we can talk privately for a moment."

I walked with Greg to the next room and then I returned to Helen.

"Helen, let me show you something. Here is how most people are made up (I drew the figure on page 103).

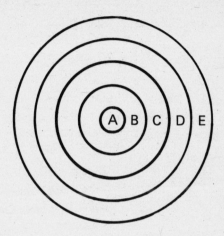

The A circle is your innermost self, the place of utmost privacy. Within it are things you rarely share with anyone at all. Then in the B circle, there are things you share with just a select few, those whom you trust totally. And so it goes out to the larger circles. By the time you get to the E circle, you are dealing with people at large. Now, sometimes people are so guarded in their expression that the drawing of their life looks like this:

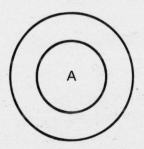

The inner part dominates. The boundaries are extremely strong. In your studies, you could compare this with the psychiatric concept of the dissociated complex."

"Right; I understand."

"Well, this is not your case at all, of course, but I wanted to show you an extreme to make the basic diagram perfectly clear. Now, we know each other well; our meeting last year was profitable, as you have already said, and now you're trusting me to help plan your marriage next June. (Then, with eyes on the first diagram completely, using a pencil to emphasize the circumference of the circle A, keeping her attention on this point exclusively) Now, tell me something from this inner circle, something you've never told anyone."

"About what . . . what kind of thing?"

(Still concentrating on the diagram) "Well, usually people keep to themselves things that relate to sex, aggression, or dishonesty. We all have private secrets about these things."

"Oh . . . I see . . ."

"Tell me something now from this inner circle of yours."

". . . well . . . lesbian fantasies . . ."

"That's normal, Helen. We both know that this is no problem to you, but you're getting married soon; tell me something from this inner circle, perhaps in relation to Greg . . ."

". . . He's not strong enough."

"Or, perhaps, you're *too* strong?"

"I see."

The key was reached, and the two of us were able to discuss her emphatic ego strengths, their shared profession, his temperament, the rigors of doctors' hours, what was expected from homelife, the role differences as doctors together and people together. Just recently, during their courtship, Greg had been unfaithful to her, and they had had a very big argument about it. Helen said: "But I know he didn't instigate it. I mean, I'm sure he was talked into it. It wasn't anything. He just sort of fell into the situation."

"You mean he's not strong enough to have gotten himself out of it?"

The pattern was clear: her strength was seen in terms of his weakness. Privately they were both worried about this juxtaposition of energies, linked harmoniously and equally for them as professionals, but disparately for them as individuals. Within her chart, Greg's affair had taken place when Saturn opposed Helen's Venus in September, 1974. The same transit would repeat itself in May, 1975, one month before the planned wedding. Venus rules her Taurus VIIth; Saturn is in her XIth, his Vth; and Venus is in her IIIrd, his Xth, point of honor. The marriage date was unalterable. The planetary configurations were difficult. Making the best of the situation, the election horoscope still showed difficulties with regard to the perspectives between them (Sun separating from a square with Pluto).

Greg returned to us and we discussed the anxieties about strength openly. These two intelligent people were working as hard as they could to bring themselves together in their relationship to one another.

The conclusion of the productive session together was focused on the meaning of perspectives within love and their busy lives together. They feared that doing the same highly specialized and demanding work would hurt their compatibility. I suggested that this was not necessarily the case, that together they were directed to the service of others professionally and that, after hours, together they could find themselves afresh on a different level. I shared with them a quote from Antoine de Saint-Exupery: "Love does not consist in gazing at each other but in looking together in the same direction." This quote, used in a parable technique, gave them a new perspective, a new level at which *to combine* strengths.

Role Playing and Reversal

Most often in counseling situations, the client needs a "shot in the arm," a boost of confidence, a stimulus to assertiveness. The astrologer represents strength, wisdom, and confidentiality. He has opportunities galore to build self-assurance within the client, in terms of the horoscope synthesis and its projection into the near future.

Dr. Lazarus writes on page 115 of *Behavior Theory and Beyond:*

People who derive benefit from therapy, regardless of the type of treatment they undergo, often state that they have become more outspoken, less inhibited, and able to stand up for their rights. For example, Storrow and Spanner (1962) reported that after short-term insight therapy, patients who described themselves as more dominant after therapy than before (i.e., "able to give orders," "manage others") also tended to describe themselves as improved.

When stressing the need for dominance, it is necessary to emphasize that the goal is not to become domineering. Similarly, the difference between assertion and aggression should also be noted, since outbursts of hostility, rage, or resentment usually denote pent-up or accumulated anger rather than the spontaneous expression of healthy emotion. Habits of emotional freedom imply the ability to give honest feedback (i.e., to show one's true feelings, and to do so in a frank and open manner). Emotional freedom opposes hypocrisy, phoniness, and deception. Contrary to popular belief, the result of emotional freedom is not alienation or increased vulnerability, but decreased anxiety, close and meaningful relationships, self-respect, and social adaptivity.

Clients with a difficulty in emotional freedom, expressing themselves in a relationship—for example, a son to a nagging father, a wife to her husband or his mother, a man to a fellow employee, etc.—can be helped tremendously if they can see the situation, the emotional exchange, operate from a different viewpoint, in a different pattern. They gain a new perspective through playing out the situation with the astrologer.

After the astrologer has heard the tale and understands the situation thoroughly, he or she sets up an enactment of the situation with the client.

After discussing different pros and cons of the arguments revealed within the abrasive relationship under consideration, perhaps creating hypothetical "What if you said" or "Suppose he were to say" situations, the astrologer suggests that enactment take place right then and there in the consultation room with the astrologer taking the place of the person in conflict with the client.

The client will usually show a timidity in going through the ordeal. But the astrologer should start right in, playing the role as understood from the preceding discussion period.

During the role-playing moments, real anger may come to the foreground from the client, since the astrologer, in playing the part, must play the part forcefully: whenever irrational anger intrudes or aggression shows itself—instead of emotionally free, frank, self-assertion—the astrologer drops out of the role and points out the statements that do nothing to illuminate the issue and only enflame the relationship. Often, it requires only an alteration of the way the emotion is spoken. For example: "You've just said I was 'crazy, out of my skull.' What if you said, 'I don't understand what you're saying. Let's make sure we're communicating clearly to each other,' or, 'When you say those things you're treating me like a child, and I don't think you really mean to.' Wouldn't that be better?"

These role-playing moments are often highly charged with energy. The astrologer must be aware of the nervous energy systems, the patience and self-worth factors, and the relationship networks involved, as seen within the horoscope. He must channel the tension into assertive self-confidence, seasoned with respect for the other person.

After the communication points are clarified, the roles can and should be reversed: the astrologer taking the role of the client, the client taking the role of the other person who represents the aggravation. In this instance, the client playing the "heavy" will play it to the hilt, since he or she knows it all too well and has played it in fantasy often. The astrologer must be a super polemicist to affect dramatically the client in the abrasive role, making points rationally and wisely, using everyday assertion instead of nagging.

Through role playing and role reversal, the client sees both sides of the tension issue and communication process. New perspective is established. The process takes only a few minutes and is well worth the rewards of objectification. Additionally, the client and astrologer reach an extremely close rapport.

These diagnostic techniques serve to illuminate the client's position within relationships. Anxiety about self-worth seems epidemic. The competitiveness within American life produces syndromes of neurotic anxiety that are not so widespread in other less competitive societies. There are many, many people, for example, who find it difficult to say something positive about someone else, to give a compliment. Often, these people say that what they *do* communicates what they should *say*. Of course, this is only half of the relationship dynamic. Actions *and* words speak loudest of all.

Self-understanding—the personal reward from Astrology—gives to self-esteem, self-perspective, emotional freedom, an assertive platform. Nothing will be lost within a relationship by the client's saying something positive about the people with whom he or she interacts. To say "that's a beautiful dress," "what a wonderful meal you cooked," "you've done a fine job," "I really enjoyed your letter last week," "our friendship is very important to me," or "I love you" can do wonders in obviating so many tiny anxieties before they accumulate into isolating frustration.

In a very real sense, the astrologer asks the client to practice *behavior modification* after self-awareness is established through the horoscope. Goals are set within time. Understanding becomes the base for strategy. The client can learn to reward himself for successful behavior modification: the astrologer finds something that delights the client, perhaps an especially fine bottle of wine on the weekend. He suggests that the client reward himself with such a purchase each weekend only after having accumulated, say, ten instances in interpersonal relationship during the week in which he has been positive, supportive. The objective is for the client to reward himself for consciously practiced behavior modification (for not losing one's temper, for not complaining about the job situation, for making someone else in particular happy every day, etc.).

Emotional freedom in good balance not only implies

the ability to demand one's own rights but also the willingness to observe, protect, and appreciate the rights of others.

5

Rationality

As thinking man has studied his self-awareness throughout history, new theories and new perspectives constantly have met his efforts. As philosophical and scientific theories accumulated, man absorbed them all. The Cartesian premise, "I think, therefore I am," has perhaps become the more easily accessible of these philosophies. It can easily follow that "thinking makes me be," and, "I am the way I think." In this line of reasoning, Shakespeare's quotation from *Hamlet* has often been cited: "There is nothing either good or bad but thinking makes it so."

Man meets the world with thought and reaction. Thought and reaction are activated by will. Philosophically, the will has been viewed in many different ways: Hegel saw the will and the knowledge it accumulated as a fount of freedom; Schopenhauer regarded the will as thoroughly evil, responsible for the suffering which "inevitably" accompanies life. There emerges from these many different views, reflecting the individually different men who formulated them, a legacy of dichotomous reasoning: everything is either good or

113

bad, positive or negative; thought and will can only be right or wrong.

Buddhism and other Asian religious philosophies suggest that by narcotizing the will, we may in the end achieve release in Nirvana or nothingness. Seeing the world as one is knowledge that conquers the will. But this communion with all can become suspension, passivity, and escape into nothingness.

In the modern era, thinking individuals in collectivities are massed sociologically, politically. The social class thinks together. The amassed wills work to make the negative positive, to right the wrong. Marxist philosophy denies the spiritual nature of the world (Hegel) and immerses itself within the materialist doctrines born in the eighteenth century: "Philosophers have only interpreted the world in various ways, the real task is to change it." The influence of this doctrine is also dichotomous in reasoning: the goal is good; if one does not agree with the doctrine, one is not on the side of progress; one is bad.

Freud phrased the polarities another way: pleasure and pain, unconscious and conscious. Sartre, in his existentialist view, took human freedom to the limit: man continuously chooses his destiny, with each new decision requiring some kind of total commitment.

All of us inherit all of these ideas and many, many more. It is very easy to go back through philosophical history and extract one philosopher's or another's way of thinking to justify with erudition one's *own* personal way of thinking, of existing. As with philosophy, a product of the human mind, individual behavior is a product of how each individual chooses to think. Religions, academia, politics, literature, drama—all take positions to the right or to the left, toward the positive or the negative, toward good or bad, interpreted personally or collectively. Even racial tension is polarized between black and white. "Either/or" is an eternal human dilemma. Astrology itself takes no such position: philosophical value judgments reside within the human will living out the horoscope.

Within this philosophical dilemma, there is always the threat of "bad" judgment—or, to avoid the dichotomous polarity, "not the best" judgment. Astrologically, this is the tension within relationship symbolized between Mars and Saturn, hot and cold, aggressive and conservative. In a counseling interview, the client's reactions express the polarity often: this force or that person is "against me," i.e., not "for" me; "who's right in this tension?"; "am I wrong to think this way?" The either-or way of thinking goes against the more rational view that thinking (and therefore reacting) is a *spectrum;* not a polarity. Perhaps a thought is not positive or negative, but has a position upon a spectrum of 0 to 100 per cent, has a "tentative truth value" upon a spectrum of what's appropriate for the individual (See S. I. Hayakawa, *Language in Thought and Action,* Harcourt, Brace & World, New York, 1964).

Using the tentative truth-value spectrum in counseling often exposes the fallacies of dichotomous reasoning. For example, in reference to the husband-wife tensions in the case studied on page 55:

Client: My wife is always bitching, always putting me down. She says that I always do the wrong thing.

Astrologer: What do you say to her when she comes on so strong?

Client: I tell her she's wrong. I try to reason with her, but I never get anywhere.

Astrologer: Well, when you tell her she's wrong, you're really disagreeing with her totally, aren't you?

Client: Of course I am! What else should I do!?

Astrologer: But then the argument just see-saws back and forth, doesn't it? You're no good. You're wrong. No, I'm not. Yes, you are.

Client: Yeah. It gets so bad I just have to leave.

Astrologer: Now, look: what if, instead of entirely disagreeing with her, you asked her, "Would you say I bother you more or less 72 per cent of the time?" You would be breaking up the opposition within the argument. Each of you would gain a perspective about how severe the upset is—and there is even a little humor here that does wonders!

This rational technique accentuates the perspective of how a person is thinking (therefore existing). So very often, one does not say what one thinks or doesn't think while saying. Under tension, this *ir*rationality denies the characteristic presentation of individual identity.

Astrologically, the rational part of man is Saturn: the disciplined organization of self within time, the super-ego.

Relationship with the energy represented by Mars is essential for the rationally composed identity to gain developmental energy, the will to live (Volume IX). Development is life's biggest challenge. With Mars' relationship to Saturn, man is especially challenged to react wisely (not rightly or wrongly) within the spectrum of personal development already established by him at that moment in time.

Of course, the nervous system invigorates, the fantasy system permeates, idealism leads. All dimensions of the horoscope are constantly involved within the rational process of thinking, reacting, existing, becoming.

Dichotomous reasoning extends itself to the accumulation of beliefs. The belief profile separates one individual from another: "I believe things should be this way, and she believes things should be another way. We just can't seem to get together." Perhaps "beliefs" is too ultimate a word. Indeed, it implies total awareness of attitude, i.e., 100 per cent on the truth-value spectrum, but in precluding the flexibility of tentativeness, it is too rigid and unyielding for a relationship between two different individuals. In relationship, learning about what another thinks and sharing what one thinks oneself softens tensions, blends spectra.

Seeing the other side of things (the Libran strength) breaks down for man the tendency to overgeneralize in order to define the self's position to the maximum; e.g., all politicians are crooks, all Democrats are shysters, women are lousy drivers, Astrology is for kooks. Sharing one's position and learning another's *do not intrude upon the self*. Rather, the self is more clearly defined through exposure, enriched by amplification, supported and remembered through relationship.

In counseling situations, this rational view is often overlooked. The client will be overconcerned about others' opinions (especially with the Moon in the XIth and under press, or the XIth, IXth, and VIIIth Houses activated strongly through tenancy, aspect networks, and/or dispositor dynamics), about public opinion, about keeping up with others. Many people work to please everyone all the time. The astrologer must present the rational view of existence and interaction: "other individuals, like you yourself, have expectations very different from your own. Statistically, some people are bound not to appreciate you as much as you would hope."

Closely related here is the awareness gained from explaining that "others may not appreciate you for a variety of reasons. Perhaps you remind them of someone else who really was at odds with them; someone who looked like you, had your name, worked in your job with them before you did, etc. You've got to understand this and not take it personally. Nothing has happened to really hurt you. You just *feel* hurt. Life doesn't stop. You simply have to revise your thinking, plan a little strategy, rise above the situation. Actually, others, just as we all do, sometimes react irrationally. So-and-so's not liking you doesn't mean that there is anything wrong with you. You just don't represent what so-and-so needs or expects at this time. Why don't we look at the situation very carefully.

What need does this relationship fulfill for you? What are you giving to so-and-so? What are your points of tension? Why should it be an either/or situation?"

The opinions of others, when not understood rationally, often are involuted, becoming depressing self-judgment. A symptom of this anxiety often takes the form of self-deprecation: a person will say, "I'm really stupid," or, "My life has been just plain dumb." There is a very beneficial therapy in changing the overgeneralized statement and internalized feeling to, "You really *mean to say* that you have done many stupid things, as we all have. Making mistakes is the only way we really learn to use what we know," or, "Your life is certainly not 'just plain dumb'; you've raised children, made many people happy, learned much about life, done good work. Maybe some dumb things have happened, but that's only normal. Look here, a list of the happy times we've discovered in your past proves this." The astrologer *can* make a value judgment in these instances: "Yes, I agree that *was* a terrible thing you did seven years ago. But that's in the past. You've learned from it. What does it mean for you *today?*"

Another symptom of the polarized value anxieties is the statement heard so often, "I am *only* a housewife," or, "I'm just an employee in a huge corporation." The real source of this irrationally thought-out statement about self-image is usually inadequate or interrupted education (usually a strong square relationship with the ruler of the IXth). Goals have perhaps never been formulated, a wrong job choice has complicated the situation, and/or ideals have disappeared. Individuals become apologetic about themselves, their thoughts, their possessions, their relationships. As much as possible, the astrologer must bring out of the core situation a rational awareness of what has been learned to that point in time: perhaps from a business collapse one has learned that his or her financial ability needs expert support in the next venture; in any relationship crisis, one learns to be more careful next time; one sees how important education is and studies the opportunity to catch up through avocational study, adult education programs, etc.

Throughout counseling, the astrologer is helping the client *to modify attitudes,* expressions of emotion, statements of thought. With intensified Virgo and Gemini concerns, the need to modify value-judgment rationale and technique is often very important. So much of interpersonal exchange is in the form of criticism. All too often, the voicing of these attitudes is condemnatory rather than assertively, lovingly constructive. Throughout dialogue, fantasy diagnosis, role playing, projection, and all objectification techniques, the astrologer must be keenly aware of these irrationally expressed thoughts. Here is a list of typical irrational statements that foster anxiety within relationships and within the self and usually take the form of destructive criticism:

destructive: "You're absolutely stupid."
constructive: "That was a stupid thing you did."

destructive: "You simply don't care about me at all."

constructive: "What you've done doesn't show that you care."

destructive: "Shut up."
constructive: "We really shouldn't talk like this."

destructive: "He's totally incompetent."
constructive: "What he's done isn't up to par."

destructive: "You're ugly."
constructive: "That hair color doesn't do you justice."

destructive: "You're so damn clumsy."
constructive: "Oops. The milk is spilled; let's clean it up."

Destructive criticism attacks the *whole* person irrationally. The conversion to constructive criticism discharges the feeling, yet diverts the attack from the whole individual and allows him a way out, a possibility for redemption. In a very short while, the client can learn to modify expression of attitudes, to think rationally before speaking, and alleviate anxiety considerably in day-to-day life.

Often, a person will say, "I understand the whole thing intellectually, but I can't accept it emotionally." This is a conflict between cognition and response: the response might be automatic, conditioned throughout years of repetition (irrational anger at a parent's suggestion, for example); or the response may indicate that cognition is in fact *not* complete, that understanding is not thorough, that perspective is not established. This brings us back to the premise of rational awareness: "as you think so shall you feel;" or, " 'Tis but saying so makes it so." Psychologists (Tolman, Lewin, Ellis) have charted the process this way: the stimulus (A) does *not* proceed directly to the response (C). In between there is a cognitive area (B), the thought area, that in sequence stimulates the whole reaction process: A-B-C.

For example, a client's depression might be explained by this statement: "Because I lost my job." The client states the response (C) directly from the stimulus (A). He has neglected (B), his cognition, his understanding of the situation at (A). Inspection of (B) can be extremely revealing: perhaps the man was never really happy in that job; the break from the job gives him an opportunity to get into the right direction at the right time. In the anxiety of the moment, he has forgotten the rational perspective and grounding of his understanding of the situation. Studying the A-B-C sequence, in relation to the astrological behavior pattern and the time pattern in progressions and transits, brings great insight into the changed situation.

Another example: "I'm crushed because my boyfriend left me." Again, the process is directly to (C) from (A). (B) must be studied. What is this woman telling herself at (B)? Perhaps something like, "I'm rejected. I wasn't good enough. I'm less a woman. I failed, and I'll probably never have another chance." Immediately, it is obvious that her thoughts have determined her reaction.

Of course, the event at (A) means nothing in terms of the thoughts framed at (B). Surely, something was learned from the relationship and the break-up. The astrologer, working with the client, can change the thoughts at (B), modify them rationally, and thus alter the response at (C).

The major lesson learned from these very instructive attitude- and behavior-modification techniques is that the client can remember the process independently and, in the face of tension in the future, ask himself the question, "Am I responding rationally? Do (A), (B), and (C) line up in the way best for me within my self-understanding and anticipated development?"

In summation, there are sixteen points of view, rational maxims, that cover the great majority of client concerns. Each astrologer can adjust his or her own list, of course, but the point here is that making classic human concerns rational works wonders in administering helpful counsel:

1. Ascendant, Sun and Moon focus, Saturn transits: *when things are not as one wants them to be, one should guard against overgeneralization and overreaction.* Frustration is one thing, anger and depression are quite something else. Frustration gaining rational perspective becomes developmental energy for self-improvement.

2. IInd House focus by tenancy, networks, rulership, etc.: *it is far better to determine self-worth less by external achievement and competence than by internal self-understanding.*

3. IIIrd House focus; network of the inner-will planets:

nearly all feelings of unhappiness are due to internal thoughts and not to the events themselves. The event may be upsetting, but the individual need not be "very upset."

4. IVth House, its axis, the rulers, etc.: *parental guidance is naturally essential, but the objective of parental caring is ideally the child's benefit and not the parents'.* Many individuals become frustrated as they live within the mold cast for them by the parents. Saturn's symbolic focus upon individual ambition must separate itself from parental possession in order for the personality to find its own definition.

Everyone's past history has inevitably influenced present behavior; it need not *continue* in influence, direction, and effect.

5. Vth House: *love given issues from a stabilized self-concept; giving attracts receiving.* "I cannot begin to love until the 'right' situation presents itself" betrays an insecure self-appraisal. An ideal situation is created to preclude challenge to the self's ability to love and to give.

6. VIth House: *a sense of service does not diminish self-definition; rather, service and cooperation lead to the formation of relationships.* A reaction of any kind made independently of the other party's whole self-organization breaks up cooperative relationship and introduces the possibility of social, mental, or physical underachievement, illness.

7. VIIth House: *the concept of "bad behavior" by others and retaliatory action by the individual should be eliminated.* The rational concepts of human fallibility and learning from past mistakes should replace condemnation or rebound-feelings of self-blame. How one meets the

world of others is reflected in how others see the individual. The two concepts should be congruent.

8. VIIIth House: *when the self-concept is secure and understood, working within the self-concepts of others is not threatening.* The structure of relationships establishes the value of cooperation to the extent that the secure individual dedicates energies to growth and development through others.

9. IXth House: *constantly taking the easy way out, losing perspective of the self, produces laziness, boredom, and fear.* An absence of squares, an accent upon mutability, Jupiter oriental (Volume IX) and retrograde, or insulated by networks of trines and sextiles, correspond to an individual for whom others do the thinking. One may think one has all the answers, while too easily functioning only as an echo.

10. Xth House: *any determined quest for perfection or absolute control over one's position in life is likely to produce panic and inefficiency during pressure periods.* Often, this ideal is inherited from a forceful parent. The individual is rarely speaking from his or her own self-awareness perspective; the means to achieve a goal become functionally autonomous and exist as an end in themselves. With the self-concept challenged or veiled in time of tension, the rigidly perfected means can be unresourceful and ineffective.

11. XIth House: *it is not absolutely necessary for an individual to receive love from all significant other people in life.* The object is to separate what is *desirable* from what is *necessary*.

A second rational maxim for XIth House concerns:

There is no value in becoming upset about friends' troubles, tensions, problems, and disturbances. This does not preclude helpfulness and caring, but works to protect the self's own organization from others' upsets, especially when an individual has the Moon within the XIth House.

12. XIIth House; Mercurial nervous networks: *anxiety and dread about pending events are emotionally debilitating and destructive.* The individual invariably suffers more before the fact than after. It undermines constructive self-assertion and introduces self-limitation.

13. Networks of square aspects: *progress is impossible without tension.* Avoiding tension brings passivity. This concept applies to those who are overdisciplined in reaction, too hard upon themselves, and those who flee from responsibility. *Welcoming tension,* with rational self-understanding, introduces developmental potential.

14. A Grand-Trine complex: *routine maintenance of the status quo inhibits growth.* An individual's need and behavior patterns, when routinized and operating within a closed circuit, require input *and* outlet for maximum development. The "windows" must be opened.

15. Multiple oppositions: *competing points of focus in life should be consolidated in understanding for most efficient application of developmental energies.* Different needs should be organized with different energy values. Distillation of the reigning need (Volume V) must establish priorities within the awareness of different energy networks: the teacher who is also an artist is perhaps foremost a communicator; an individual may fashion his or her job to serve his or her religious needs; an athlete may be a nutritionist as well, working toward the promotion of

physical rehabilitation; a historian may also be a lawyer in quest of political fulfillment.

16. Extraordinary individuation pressures within development; progressed Sun square Uranus, for example: *individuation is best founded upon independence when the independence maintains perspective of relationship.* Too often, the individual yearning to be "free" loses sight of the necessity for relationship. Rationality is lost in highly focused self-awareness. Taking life into one's own hands is separatistic rather than self emphasizing.

These maxims of rational thought help the client toward behavior modification. Keyed to horoscopic synthesis and time structures, they constructively stabilize anxiety reactions, refine the cognitive process, and therefore alter attitude. The assertive, emotionally free personality is placed in a fresh perspective to meet developmental challenges in the future.

The Rational Astrologer

Rationality is the state of reasoned understanding. It is much more than description. Astrological counseling must go beyond description of symbolic structures. It must offer behavior modification within the security of thoroughly understood symbology, past and future.

Espousing this modern view in our work practically eliminates the tension surrounding how and why Astrology "works," the causality dilemma. This is no longer important. *How* and *when* a person uses Astrology *is* important.

For example, Saturn is not "a strike against

someone," as is so often stated. Saturn symbolically represents a challenge of one kind or another to an individual. Inexplicably, the position of Saturn is translated into a living dimension of behavior. The individual's behavior incredibly corresponds to the movement of this planet-symbol. So it is with all the symbols. In their "natures" symbolically, they are constant. Synthesis among them creates corresponding individual differences. *But it is always the human being—not the planets—who makes things happen.*

To serve the human being—and not the horoscope—the astrologer translates symbolic deductions in terms of needs. These needs motivate action, the individual behaves in different ways to fulfill these needs, and the process of becoming takes place. The horoscope does not live, just as a portrait does not live; but an individual must.

At all times then, when discussing the horsocope in consultation, when sharing rational understanding, we must know that sensitive, perceptive, and thorough communication is our foremost responsibility. Our communication must be effective to be of service, must be adjusted to different individuals at different levels, with different needs, in different states of tension. Jargon-inflated descriptions have no value at all. They must be translated into terms of needs and behavior and be placed within time. Through the techniques of objectification, the client sees his or her life needs and behavior clearly, in non-judgmental perspective. The cognitive processes are analyzed and behavior modification takes place. The process of becoming, the reason for being, is refined.

Several months ago, a woman telephoned me for an appointment. She was the client of another astrologer in town who had moved away. I urged the woman to telephone her astrologer long distance since she would surely have acquaintance with the case in depth and could be helpful quickly. The woman insisted that I see her instead.

The woman, "Joan," was an executive in an employment agency and had many local government contacts. She was divorced, with a child, and was contemplating an important job shift from the one field into the other. She was tall, strong, a Capricorn, and seemed very poised and self-assured. Her horoscope reflected the overall strength and the excellent conditions of the challenging present.

But Joan was quite distraught. Our dialogue revealed a totally needless anxiety: "I'm so afraid. I don't know what to do: my karma is killing me." It became clear that her astrologer had spent much time discussing Joan's karma. One wonders how a discussion of karma could be of any value, except academic or philosophical. It certainly was debilitating for Joan in the face of practical circumstances.

Perhaps the astrologer used a jargon description called karma for descriptive deductions that she could not translate into behavior. Perhaps she talks about karma to all her clients, fitting each person irrationally to one mode of delineation and communication.

Joan became increasingly aggrieved. The fear of karma was very real. There was no sense in discussing any other concept of karma to help with *her* concept of karma. I immediately planned to distract her, to objectify her fears to an extreme, to blow them up to the ridiculous (page 46). I took a piece of white paper and interrupted her: "Joan, please, let's digress for a moment. I want you to work with me here on this paper. I want to draw a floor plan of your house. You'll see why in a moment."

With as much persuasion and leadership as I could bring to the dialogue, I elicited from her the downstairs plan of her home: the windows, the interior walls, the kitchen, fireplace, stairwells to the cellar and to the second floor . . . all the details. I drew them carefully. Soon she was immersed in the plan, getting everything exact.

I took a second piece of paper and, with her, did the same thing for the second floor. She was cooperating totally: "Then over here (pointing to the drawing) is my daughter's room, about 10′ by 13′, I think. The door opens in, and the large closet over here . . . etc."

Just as we were completing the floor plan, I pretended to be perplexed: "Wait a minute, Joan, I don't think this is quite right."

"Yes, it is. There are the three bedrooms, the baths, the dressing room, the . . . "

"No, there's one room missing."

"There ISN'T!"

"Yes there is, Joan: where does *karma* sleep?"

The shock was tremendous, and in the space of about five seconds dissolved into laughter. Wondrously, karma was gone. The objectification and diversion had taken the debilitating concept to a ridiculous extreme. The irrational perspective was shattered and a rational perspective took its place. Her cognitive process was changed "in the twinkling of an eye." With calm, comfort, and freedom, Joan and I were able to go right on to her strategies for the job change. She called a few weeks later to tell of success and, in response to my question about karma, practically laughed me off the telephone!

Astrology longs to be recognized as a science. But whether or not Astrology is a science is *unimportant* in the view of this volume since it is the human being who makes Astrology work and *not* the planets or their symbols. Religion is not a science; nor is artistic composition, etc. Rather, it is the human element that justifies the knowledge. If Astrology were a science, then all our lives would be ordered and wise, with constant fulfillment of needs and potentials. Everyone would be an astrologer. If religion were scientific, there would be only one. Every astrologer searches for "magic measurements," some measurements within the horoscope that will reliably respond to scientific method, i.e., correspond to the same response every time in every case. Indeed, some measurements approach this predictability, but the "magic measurements" are found *within* the astrologer, discovered through sharing and studying the lives of the individuals whom Astrology serves. The magic is in the contact between Astrology and human being: both are transformed in a recognition of individuality within time.

The more astrologers respect the individuality factor of astrological application and have faith that the individual knows his or her horoscope best, the more dignity will be brought to Astrology. Blanket predictions will fall away in their own overgeneralized, irrational absurdity. The assertion of the will will rise in rational perspective and emotional freedom. The astrologer will truly become the medium between divine endowment and individual fulfillment.

Nature's organization guides the astrologer's art and accumulated knowledge (science). There may be eternal questions about the scope of aspect orbs, about House systems. The answers to these questions cannot yet be the same for every individual. (Yet, the gifted researchers within Astrology deserve all our support and gratitude.) The answers to these questions are now within the will and behavior structure of the individual who possesses the horoscope. For example, if a planet is on the cusp of an interior House and the astrologer knows that in another House system this planet would be over the Sign line into the next House and have a different significance, there is no need to worry about which House system is "right" or "wrong." This is dichotomous thinking. The answer is found simply by asking the client a question about this point in synthesis. The client knows best the behavior that corresponds to the astrological deductions. If the question is about an orb of aspect reference, again, a question to the client will provide the answer. Time and time again, individuals with assertive wills and rational cognitive processes will reach beyond even the widest "established" orb to creative a supportive aspect between two symbolic energy dimensions, to make things happen in a specific way at a specific time. (We will explore in Volume XII of this series how the will can actually alter the horoscope.)

None of these difficulties remain when the astrologer serves through a two-sided sharing with the client. As soon as a one-sided performance takes place, the dynamism that is life is made static; the client's will is denied; individuality is lost by being adjusted to the perspective of an astrologer's routinized way of seeing things.

In astrological consultation, *two* individuals share together to gain illumination. The symbols themselves eventually mean nothing as they gain translation into life. The human elements discover a path and adjust progress along it. The whole is a recognition of the "all-pervasive creative principle" presented to us by Paul Tillich.

In personal correspondence received today, the much loved astrologer Isabel Hickey wrote: "It's the Light the people follow whoever the bearer be." She refers to the meaning and understanding accomplished *through* Astrology and astrologers, to the illumination of self within the life-gift of the Creator.

In the end, each of us must see the Light first before we can follow it. Within ourselves, we must find stimulus, create rational understanding of it, and construct attitudes that will respect the illumination in others. We need open windows to let inspiration in and out. We need room inside us for the discovery and development of magic measurements. From stores of knowledge other than Astrology, we need so much more, to enrich our awareness continually, as individuals and as practitioners. How full we must be to presume to serve!

Appendix

Example Horoscopes for Organization and Synthesis

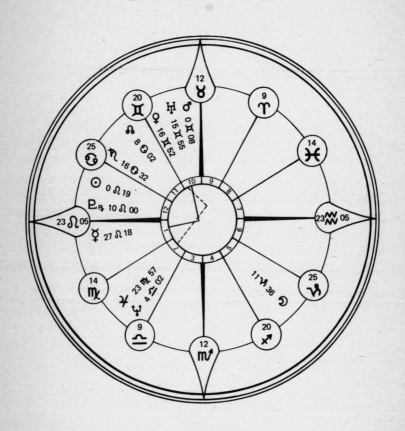

Female school teacher at age twenty-six. Self-worth anxiety: Leo Sun in XII conjunct retrograde Pluto; rising Mercury in Leo, ruling the IInd, square Mars in X, ruler of IX, others' opinions. Saturn in Cancer in XI adds the need for love and acceptance, especially through the work situation (ruler of VI and VII); there is a keen awareness of the Capricorn Moon's needs to administer the self, focused in V, self-speculation, love given, educational activity. Parental roots of the problem: Venus, ruler of X, in X and square Jupiter in II (Mercury disposes of both Venus and Jupiter); Pluto rules Scorpio and is with the Sun in XII. Note the egocentric defensive orientation of the whole chart. On the job, she allied herself with administrative politics in order to gain behind-the-scenes ascendancy.

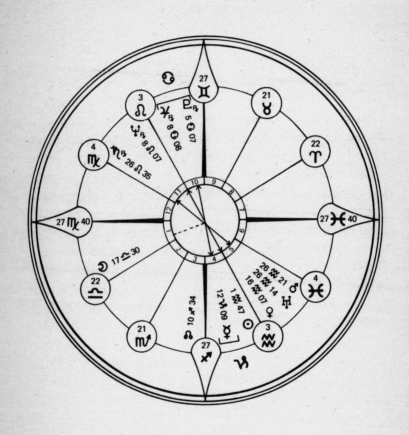

Female physical therapist at age fifty-three. Great need for love (Saturn in XI opposed Uranus-Mars conjunction in V), dependency upon others' recognition of her own unusual way of doing things (Mars rules VIII; Neptune rules VII; Venus, gaining opposition to Saturn, rules IX; Mercury rules X and XII and is in opposition with Jupiter and Pluto, both retrograde in X; the Sun opposes Neptune in XI). The rulers of the entire southern hemisphere are under strong tension; all planets above the horizon are retrograde.

She was married to an extremely powerful man who paid her little attention. He died suddenly, and the woman fantasizes to an occult extreme that their love was true and good (Neptune in XI within the networks, ruling the VIIth), although she was repeatedly victimized by his unfaithfulness and neglect. Her legacy of inferiority feelings (Saturn retrograde, Jupiter retrograde, rulers of IV; Saturn is dispositor of Mercury in IV, ruler of X; the Moon square with Jupiter and Pluto, the Moon ruling Cancer intercepted in X) is easily linked with early parental upbringing in Germany: the rigid masculine emphasis conflicted with her need to be herself (Moon in I; Vth House tension); her marriage to a man from the same mold.

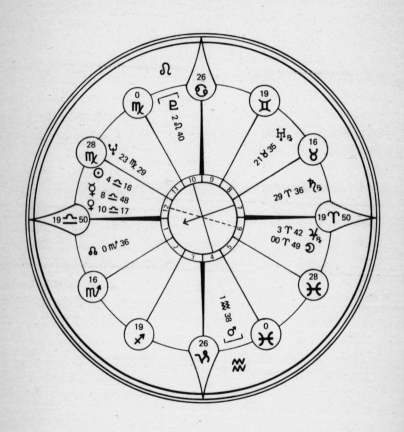

Male ballet dancer at age thirty-three. Extreme ego anxiety taken on through the mother, emphasized by her early death, and reflected through a social insecurity (retrograde Saturn in VII within the T Cross, with Pluto-Mars discharged *upon the nodal axis* into the Ascendant. Saturn's position over the sign line in Aries also emphasizes the ego component, echoed by the Moon in Aries). The personality is heavily debilitated through the Full-Moon opposition placing the Sun in the XIIth along with Mercury and Venus. Neptune rules the Vth and is in the XIth, the fantasy element of love-received in compensation, from individuals and from the public audience at ballet performances. The Moon in VI (the job conditions) is in conjunction with Jupiter retrograde, co-ruler of V. The man is a homosexual.

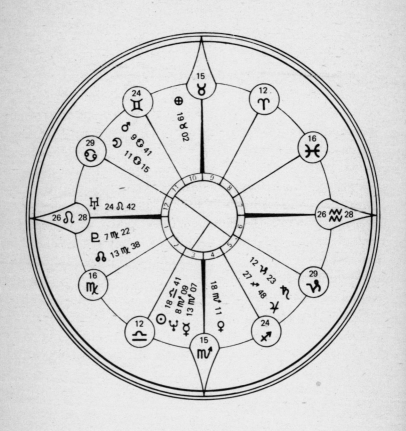

Boy at age eleven: the T Cross in Cardinal Signs dominates the horoscope. There is a tremendous need for friends, for home security, for communication skill. At such an early age, charged by a precocious pride (Leo Ascendant with Uranus rising trine Jupiter in Sagittarius), the energy reservoir causes great tension internally, literally wracking the system (Saturn rules Capricorn on VI; the Moon rules Cancer on XII). The boy is a chronic asthmatic. The personality projection as an adult will be so strong, probably in overcompensation for the debilitated early years, as to attract friends and even result in his championing the underdog, as a man of letters, keenly aware of social injustices (Pluto sextile Neptune and Mercury in III with the Libra Sun, and sextile Mars in XI, ruler of IX; Uranus rising trine Jupiter in V; Saturn in Capricorn). In his wealthy home with a much older doctor father and mother, he behaves and is treated like a prince.

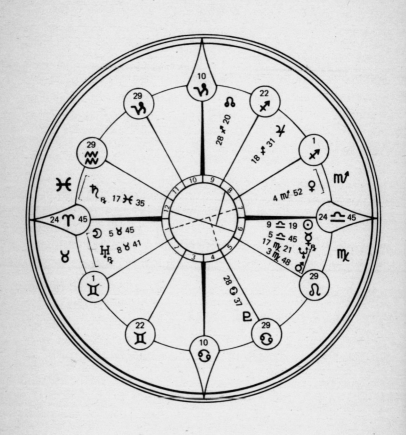

Male homosexual waiter at thirty-seven. The T Cross involving Moon-Uranus opposed Venus, the axis squared by Pluto over the Sign line in the Moon's Sign, Cancer, focuses attention greatly upon the sex profile: the Moon rules Cancer on the Vth and is conjunct retrograde Uranus; Venus is in Scorpio, rules the VIIth, disposes of the Moon, Uranus, the Sun, and retrograde Mercury, and is itself disposed of by Pluto. This T Cross discharges into the XIth, ruled by Saturn, and Saturn is retrograde in the XIIth within another T Cross: opposed Neptune, the axis squared by Jupiter.

The man lives with his lover in a restaurant business owned by the latter. The problem for him is to find his own way. His sexual preference crystallized when Saturn-Mars transited natal Venus as Neptune transited the seventh cusp in January, 1954. Earlier, his family and home were totally broken up during the war in Germany, as Saturn and Mars transited the Ascendant.

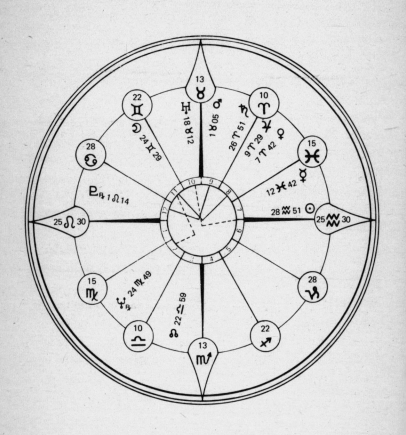

Housewife at age thirty-three. With the Sun in VII, ruling the Ascendant, squared by Uranus, ruler of the VIIth, the woman is bound to have strong, enduring tension within relationships, specifically with her husband. The Moon, ruler of XII, is trine the Sun and square Neptune: she has a vast network of friends who support all her complaints, and she drinks to cover her awareness of the troubles (Mercury, dispositor of Neptune and the Moon, is in mutual reception with Neptune retrograde in II, is square the Moon and sextile Uranus). The ego is extremely defensive and torn between acquiescence and strong aggression (Saturn in Aries in conjunction with Mars). The IXth House emphasis, with Mars square Pluto, suggests a self-perspective totally lost within the marriage. Her husband makes every decision for her (her IXth is his IIIrd). He is a homosexual (reading her chart for him; all the tensions keyed to her XIth, his Vth; the importance of Mercury).

The woman was counseled to see reality through sober eyes and to divorce her husband in accordance with strongly favorable transits and progressions focused upon the progressed Sun trine Pluto, nearing Full Moon.

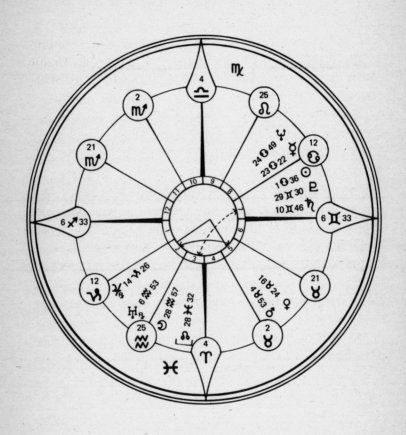

Theatre librarian, lesbian, at age fifty-nine. The only tension network within the horoscope is the Mars-Uranus square between the Vth and the IInd. Jupiter, ruler of the Ascendant, is retrograde in Capricorn in the IInd and is trine Venus, ruler of the Vth and the Xth, in the Vth. She had always wanted to be a performer. There is not enough drive and developmental tension to fulfill this. She now works as an information researcher in a music library (Venus synthesis; Moon in the IIIrd) and is extremely content. Her whole life was caught up with love for theatrical charade, meeting important theatrical people (Pluto oriental in VII). She presents herself to the public as if she were at a masquerade party (Mercury, ruler of VII, is conjunct Neptune, both disposed of by the Moon). The Moon in Aquarius makes her needs eccentric and novel (trine Pluto). Just being around theatrical people and friends who are successful fulfills her needs (Pluto rules XI).

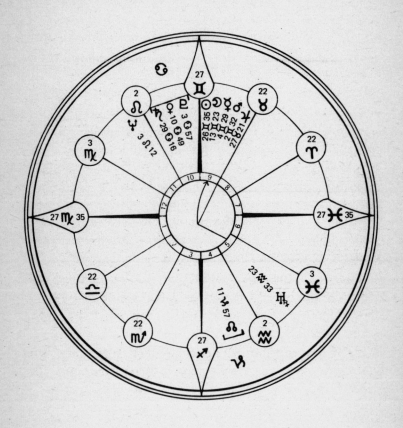

Divorced woman at age fifty-four. The horoscope has only one square and no opposition among the planets. The Angles are all Mutable. Only the trine from Uranus to the Moon and Sun eases the link between hemispheres. The woman speaks several languages, talks knowledgeably and incessantly about many things (Mars-Mercury conjunction in Gemini, Gemini Sun, Moon, and Midheaven), but her nerves are totally frayed (Mercury rules Ascendant, Sun squares Ascendant) from an intensely hypercritical, unending attack upon her husband who simply abandoned her a few years ago. Her overreaction refers clearly to the IXth House with the sextile of Mars-Mercury to Neptune in XI, disposed of by the Sun, Neptune ruling the VIIth. She talks openly and much about her sexual frustrations (the links with Uranus retrograde in V in its own Sign), but resists doing anything about the frustration because of her upbringing (Venus in Cancer conjunct the nodal axis in the parental axis).

She lives life through her children (V) and her friends (XI), who view her as almost a comic figure (Neptune).

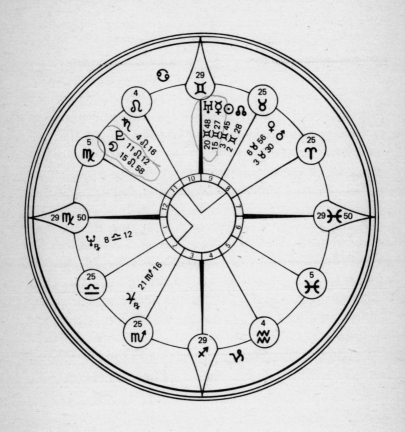

Male tradesman at age twenty-seven. The crisis is really a tremendous need for love, for friends (Saturn and Moon in the XIth); but the complex is under the tension of his not being able to express emotion to attract this love and friendship, indeed, of his inability to make value judgments at all, about self-esteem and reactions to the opinions of others (Saturn square with the Venus-Mars conjunction in the VIIIth, Venus ruling Libra on II and Taurus on IX, Venus disposing of Mars and of Neptune rising).

The tension has its roots in an extremely tyrannical father figure: Saturn and its own symbolism and also as ruler of Capricorn intercepted in the IVth; echoed by the Moon's square to Jupiter retrograde in the IInd, ruling Sagittarius on the IVth. There are further indications of the parental tension: Mercury, ruler of X, in conjunction with Uranus and semi-square Mars; the Moon ruling Cancer intercepted in the Xth.

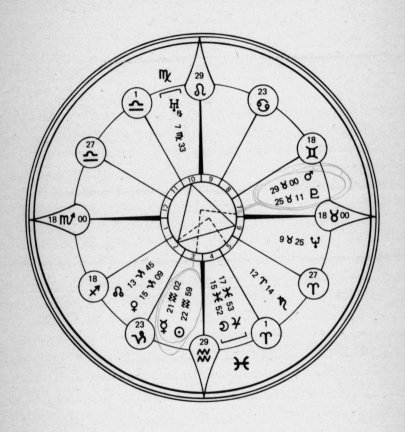

Labor leader, orator John L. Lewis (12 February 1880, 00:40 A.M.; Lucas, Iowa). The stocky, barrel-chested, bushy-haired powerhouse, Lewis, fits the Scorpio Ascendant perfectly. His public projection was overwhelmingly tyrannical (Mars conjunct Pluto in VII, squared by Mercury-Sun in III). His Earth Grand Trine (without the Sun or Moon) operated as a grounding for his unyielding demands for recognition of the coal miners and labor in general. His emotionality was totally one-sided (Venus square Saturn) and gave an awesome ministerial support to his electrifying oratory (Saturn sextile Mercury-Sun conjunction in Aquarius in the IIIrd).

Yet, we wonder about the private man inside this historical figure: Moon-Jupiter conjunction in Pisces, intercepted in the IVth, sextile Venus and sextile Pluto-Mars. Somehow, was he privately self-vindicating in an awareness of mission, of some higher responsibility during his life and work (the Moon rules IX; Jupiter rules II; Neptune is dispositor of the Moon and Jupiter; Venus is dispositor of Neptune, rules VII and XII, and is exalted in Pisces, the Sign holding the Moon and Jupiter)?

Supplementary Reading List

Ellis, Albert. *Reason and Emotion in Psychotherapy.* New
   York: Lyle Stuart, 1962.
Hayakawa, S. I. *Language in Thought and Action.* New
   York: Harcourt, Brace & World, 1964.
Lazarus, Arnold A. *Behavior Therapy and Beyond.* New
   York: McGraw-Hill Book Company, 1971.
Rudhyar, Dane. *An Astrological Study of Psychological
   Complexes and Emotional Problems.* Lakemont,
   Georgia: CSA Press, 1974.

An intriguing voyage
from the earth to the stars . . . and beyond

ASTROLOGY: MUNDANE, ASTRAL, OCCULT

Volume XI of *The Principles and Practice of Astrology*

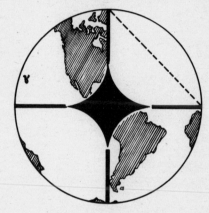

Three Books in One!

Mundane Astrology—astrology's most difficult area made almost as easy as natal astrology. Specialized meanings of planets, houses, signs; corroboration through overlaying horoscopes of leaders, parties, sub-cultures, other nations—all viewed against an historical backdrop. An in-depth case-study of the Arab-Israeli conflict. Astrological phenomenology: ingresses, eclipses, great conjunctions and comets.

Astral Astrology—a succinct introduction to the major stars, plus an account of how they are used in natal, mundane, horary and medical astrology.

The Occult—the horoscope as a mandala revealing man's orientation toward completeness; the mysterious "finger of God"; the triune subdivisions within each sign; the "part of spirit"; extensive treatment of the Law of Karma and the cycle of reincarnation; degree symbolism; finding sensitivity to the occult in the chart.

The Principles and Practice of Astrology
for home study and college curriculum
by Noel Tyl
in twelve volumes

I. **Horoscope Construction**

Here is an unrivaled explanation of the construction of a horoscope. All time and position corrections are made maximally clear. A totally self-contained volume, with tables and practice horoscope blanks. Contents include: calculating the time of birth—step-by-step guidance, use of materials and examples; measuring the houses—what they are, how they're placed; the calligraphy—the symbols of astrology, meaning of the signs, illustrative birthdays of famous people; placing the planets—measuring planetary movement, test horoscopes; calculation review—special time problems explained; the Sun and the signs—the Sun as the key, Sun Sign interpretations, the elements, polarities, modes; the ruling planets—meaning and function of planets in the chart with sample horoscopes reviewed; the Age of Aquarius—what it is and what it means to astrologers.

II. **The Houses: Their Signs and Planets**

The rationale of house demarcation, the meanings of the signs upon each house, the planets' significance in every house; derivative house readings.

III. **The Planets: Their Signs and Aspects**

A full expansion of the elements and modes in a refreshingly modern style; the significance of every planet within every sign; the reading of aspects and dignities "at a glance"; the suggested meanings of all major aspects and Sun-Moon combinations. An invaluable master reference book for horoscope interpretation.

IV. Aspects and Houses in Analysis

Analytical synthesis technique presented through many examples, showing hemisphere emphasis, retrogradation patterns, the grand trine, the grand square, the T square in complete explanation, the lunar nodal axis, parallels of declination, and the part of fortune; the "law of naturalness." A volume devoted totally to the art of synthesis.

V. Astrology and Personality

Never before presented: an explanation of psychological theories of personality translated into astrological terms and technique! The theories of Kurt Lewin, Carl Jung, Henry Murray, Abraham Maslow, Erich Fromm, Alfred Adler and Sigmund Freud; and astrological glossary of psychological terms and personality traits.

VI. The Expanded Present

An introduction to prediction, an analysis of the time dimension in astrology; application and separation of aspects, "rapport" measurements, secondary progression, primary directions, "factor 7" analysis. Many examples clarify the work of astrology toward understanding change and development in personality, within free-will and fate.

VII. Integrated Transits

A definitive work, modernizing the rationale, analysis and application of transit theory, in accord with the needs and expectations of modern people. Astrology is translated into behavior with many real-life examples for every major transit. The work also includes studies of solar revolution, rectification, eclipse theory, and accidents.

VIII. Analysis and Prediction

A gallery of astrological portraits: the whole-view of astrological analysis; inspection of the past, expansion of the present, the creation of the future. Each step of deduction, analysis, and projection is presented in the sharing of real-life horoscopes: *you* become the astrologer! Radix methods, progressions, and transits are fully interpreted. In addition, there is an introduction to Horary and Electional Astrology.

IX. Special Horoscope Dimensions

Success: vocation, relocation, opportunity, elections. Sex: chart comparison, sex profile, love, homosexuality, abortion, creativity. Illness: health problems, surgery, vitality.

X. Astrological Counsel

Never before presented: a full, detailed inspection of the psychodynamics of the astrologer-client relationship, with examples showing the astrologer's consideration of the horoscope *and* the individual, bringing together the personality and its time structure for fulfillment. Difficulties analyzed, communication techniques explored.

XI. Astrology: Mundane, Astral, Occult

A fascinating voyage through the Astrology of nations, to the fixed stars, and beyond. A thorough and adventurous introduction to Mundane Astrology governing international events; Israel, Arabia, Germany, England, USA; Solar Ingresses, Great Conjunctions; the areas shared by astrology and occult studies, Sign subdivision and degree symbolism, karma and reincarnation.

XII. Times to Come

A thorough introduction to the techniques of Cosmobiology, Sidereal Astrology, and the Uranian System; their philosophical and behavioral parallels involving the art of creative compromise, remembrance of things past, and creative visualization.

**The Teaching and Study Guide
to the Principles and Practice of Astrology
by Noel Tyl
Price $15.00**

The various texts in *The Principles and Practice of Astrology* series have been acclaimed as the "finest astrological teaching books of this generation." Now those of you who want to study supplementary topics under the same masterful tutelage will find in *The Teaching and Study Guide* many of the topics and refinements of technique excluded from or only touched on in the series, in order to achieve lucidity of presentation: the rationales for the various house systems; advanced derivative house reading; the Naiboda, Sepharial, and Simmonite refinements of predictive techniques; key-cycle solar returns; the harmonic theory of aspects; the composite chart; further refinements in mundane theory, such as the application of critical aspects to world capitals and leaders through geographical coordinates; plus the whole gamut of sophisticated *and simplified* measurement techniques.

In addition, you have the benefit of an additional perspective on material already covered in the series. The sexual profile in the horoscope, for example, is further clarified through an in-depth study of the "homosexual matrix." Delineation techniques are illuminated when you are show how to derive planet-sign, house-sign, aspect-planet, etc., capsule notations on your own—rather than simply accepting textbook recipes. By being assisted in understanding the rationale behind delineation, you come to a greater understanding of just how astrology works, and *you become your own astrologer!*

If you are interested in using the book to teach others, you will find a wealth of material: lesson plans, study questions, classroom exercises, dramatic classroom presentations that make even tedious subjects like computation exciting. If you are interested in further teaching *yourself*, you will find it an invaluable supplement to the series.

Available through Llewellyn Publications (Box 3383-PPA, St. Paul, Minnesota 55165) or your local bookdealer.

The Horoscope as Identity   **Price $10.00**

Studies in the Astrology of Sex, Ambition, and Identity within modern, freer times.   **by Noel Tyl**

What the publisher says:

If this is truly a New Age that we have entered, the Age of Aquarius, then there must be new things said: new interpretations of the Ancient Wisdom of which we are the guardians.

At Llewellyn we receive an average of one manuscript every day—most of them saying nothing, some of them saying old things in new ways, some of them publishable. For a cycle of twelve years I waited to see a manuscript that said something new in astrology—and I waited in vain. I did not see a single astrological book meeting that ideal until the exact completion of that twelve-year cycle in February of 1973—and then it happened!

As far as Llewellyn is concerned, a new star was born on the day that I completed reading the manuscript of *The Horoscope as Identity*.

The author of this book actually incarnates the new influx of psychological meaning in terms of astrological practice that this Age demands. He speaks to the needs of the present and coming student of astrology and psychology combined as they should be.

This is not a book of tables, or a repetition of what is said well or poorly in so many other books. It is not a book that sees astrology as frozen in medieval times and meanings. It is a book for both the advanced student of astrology and the intelligent layman who wants to see what is really in modern astrology. It is a book for the reader who is ready to be liberated—who will be able to use the knowledge of self and this world to achieve freedom and mastery of his destiny that is the goal of all astrological and psychological analysis.

The particular value of this book is the modern understanding of Saturn in the chart, the concept of the sex-profile, and the guidance to speed-reading the horoscope. Case studies include: Albert Speer, Hitler's architect; a famous businessman (survival or death); Judy Garland.

Fifty-eight horoscope charts illustrate the text.

Small blanks for practice only; large-circle form
recommended. Order recommended blanks, style 9 (with
aspect grid), package of 100, AS5-$3.00, from Llewellyn
Publications, Box 3383, St. Paul, Minnesota 55165, or from
your local bookdealer. Other astrological tools, such as
Ephemerides, etc., may be obtained there also.

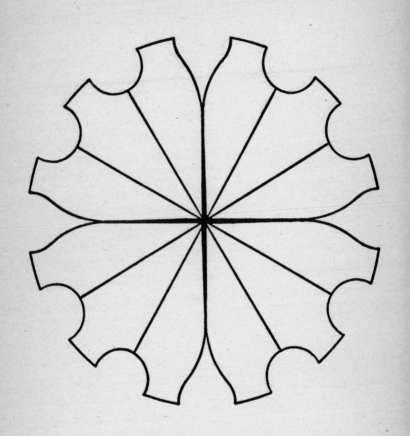

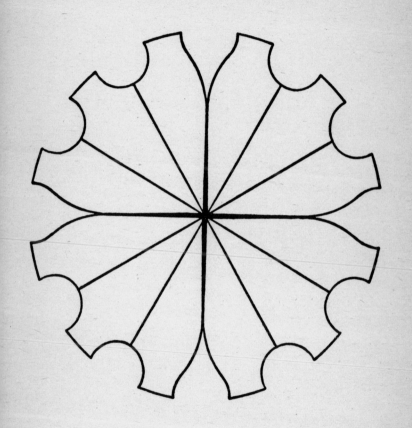

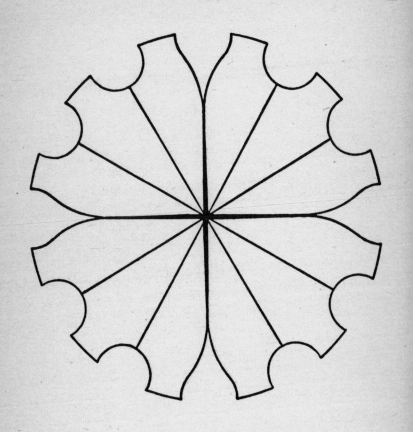

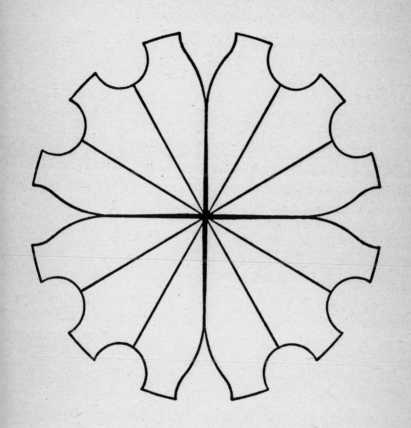